BUSINESS 5.0 PERSPECTIVES AND PEOPLE MANAGEMENT PRACTICES

TRANSFORM - TRANSITION - THRIVE

FOR FORWARD-THINKERS WHO WANT TO BE FUTURE-READY

Dr. Vijayalaxmi Moovala

Copyright © Dr. Vijayalaxmi Moovala 2024
All Rights Reserved.

ISBN 979-8-89277-788-9

This book has been published with all efforts taken to make the material error-free after the consent of the author. However, the author and the publisher do not assume and hereby disclaim any liability to any party for any loss, damage, or disruption caused by errors or omissions, whether such errors or omissions result from negligence, accident, or any other cause.

While every effort has been made to avoid any mistake or omission, this publication is being sold on the condition and understanding that neither the author nor the publishers or printers would be liable in any manner to any person by reason of any mistake or omission in this publication or for any action taken or omitted to be taken or advice rendered or accepted on the basis of this work. For any defect in printing or binding the publishers will be liable only to replace the defective copy by another copy of this work then available.

Contents

Acknowledgements 7
Introduction 9

PART 1
BUSINESS 5.0 PERSPECTIVES

1   Business 5.0 . . . . **13**

⇒   Macro-level business landscape 15

⇒   Industry-technology convergence 17

⇒   Industry convergence 17

⇒   Micro-level business landscape 18

2   Business 5.0 Leadership Framework **21**

⇒   Futuristic outlook 21

⇒   Business acuity 22

⇒   Technology savvy 23

⇒   Stakeholder centricity 23

⇒   Ingenuity 24

⇒   Authenticity 24

⇒   Mental agility 25

3   Business 5.0-6 Ps Model **27**

⇒   Purpose 28

⇒   Paradigm 29

⇒   Proactivity 31

⇒   People 32

⇒   Productivity 33

⇒   Planet 34

4   Business 5.0 Standpoints **37**

⇒   Business 5.0 mindset and skill sets......................37

⇒   Business 5.0 mindset and skill sets matrix 40

⇒   Business 5.0 learning model..........................43

⇒   Business 5.0 roadmap....................................47

⇒   Business 5.0 focus areas and actions 50

PART 2
PEOPLE MANAGEMENT

5   People Engagement. **55**

⇒   Multigenerational workforce 55

⇒   Integrated employee value proposition [IEVP] 58

⇒   Diversity, equity, inclusion and belonging [DEIB].......61

⇒   Employee well-being and mental health.................67

⇒   Professionalism and employee well-being 72

⇒   Quiet quitting and loud quitting 75

⇒   Global citizenship....................................82

6   People Enablement **85**

⇒   Metaverse 85

⇒   Cyber-technology-human blended workforce 87

⇒   People analytics 87

⇒   Knowledge management.................................90

7   People Management Practices **93**

⇒   Workforce trends.....................................93

⇒   Hybrid policies 95

⇒   Employee resourcing 96

⇒   Employee selection 98

⇒   Career development 100

⇒   Compensation 102

⇒   Employee journeys 105

⇒   Employee touchpoints.................................106

PART 3
TALENT TRENDS

8   Talent Development **113**

⇒   Key skills 113

⇒   Cybersecurity skills...........................115

⇒   New skilling 116

⇒   Learning and development trends....................119

⇒   Learning journey.............................121

⇒   Bilateral/mutual coaching 122

⇒   Role of learning and development professionals 123

9   Talent Management **127**

⇒   Talent assessment 127

⇒   Talent categorisation...........................128

⇒   Talent portfolios/Multi-specialism 130

⇒   Talent ascension 131

⇒   Talent pipelines and pathways 133

10   Business 5.0 Competency Framework....................**135**

⇒   C-suite/senior-level managers......................136

⇒   Middle-level managers 138

⇒   Junior-level managers...........................140

⇒   Non-managerial level 142

References.......................................*145*

Acknowledgements

A big thank you to those people with whom I interacted and discussed Business 5.0 trends, digital disruptions, leadership concepts and people management practices, which I am sharing with the readers through this seminal work. I appreciate my peer reviewers who provided invaluable suggestions, along with words of encouragement, to make this book happen.

My heartfelt gratitude to my family members who gave me their unconditional support throughout the writing and publishing period. A special acknowledgement to my niece, Shobana Kamalakar, for being a key decision maker in the entire process.

In-text citations are in their original format.

Introduction

The business landscape, globally, has transformed, due to Industrial Revolution 4.0, which revolutionised jobs, business models, work structures, processes, and outcomes. The business scenario that unfolded, majorly because of technological disruptions, gave way to the Business 5.0 environment, in which cyber-technology-human interface is taking precedence. The focus in Business 5.0 is on optimising employee potential and harnessing technologies for improved productivity, strategic goal achievement and economic welfare.

Organisations in Business 5.0 need to have a strategic direction considering the digital disruptions and ever-changing external influences. Strategic decisions are based on the changed business landscape, redesigned business models, repurposed culture, revamped internal systems, and alignment with the dynamic Business 5.0 environment. Turnaround strategies and ecosystem leverage, leading to stakeholder value creation, underlie success in Business 5.0. Leaders and managers, who are at the helm of these transformational processes, are empowered to give the right impetus for sustainability in the Business 5.0 environment.

People management practices with an emphasis on diversity, equity, inclusion, and belonging [DEIB], integrated employee value proposition [IEVP], employee well-being, and hybrid policies are gaining momentum. New skilling employees to be equipped with the Business 5.0 mindset and skill sets, necessary for their career growth and business success is of paramount importance to organisations. Business 5.0 brought, in its wake, a new value creation for stakeholders, in which stakeholder centricity is the focus. Organisations are witnessing changed customer preferences, and employee journeys need to be aligned for delivering the expected customer experiences and achieving planned business outcomes.

The expectations of a multigenerational workforce, marked by their differences and varied abilities, characterise the Business 5.0 environment. Considering these major influencing factors, people management practices and talent development are also changing significantly. Competency frameworks formulated for Industry 3.0 and Industry 4.0 are being replaced by Business 5.0 competency frameworks.

In conclusion, the Business 5.0 environment is marked by a cyber-technology-human interface, new skilled employees, talent trends, modified people management practices aligned to the work-life fit of employees, for the sustainable development of organisations.

PART 1

BUSINESS 5.0 PERSPECTIVES

Chapters

1   Business 5.0 13

2   Business 5.0 Leadership Framework........................ 21

3   Business 5.0-6 Ps Model 27

4   Business 5.0 Standpoints 37

| 01 | Business 5.0

The global business landscape is currently characterised by digital disruptions due to Industrial Revolution 4.0, necessitating strategic redirection, operational manoeuvres, and tactical changes aligned to the changed business scenario. Industrial Revolution 4.0, in its wake, transformed businesses and their landscape in its entirety, encompassing digitalisation, re-strategising for the changed markets, internal remodelling, and alignment with the dynamics of external influences and changes.

While many organisations and industries are still adapting to Industry 4.0, Industry 5.0 is revolutionising the business landscape. The awareness of Industry 5.0 is still not widespread. "According to the European Union, Industry 5.0 places the wellbeing of the worker at the centre of the production process and uses new technologies to provide prosperity beyond jobs and growth while respecting the production limits of the planet. In other words, at its heart, Industry 5.0 reflects a shift from a focus on economic value to a focus on societal value, and a shift in focus from welfare to wellbeing" Kraaijenbrink (2022).[1] The concept of Industry 5.0:

> Is mostly focused on the integration of humans working alongside robots and IoT devices in the automated industrial environments of the future. As opposed

to Industry 4.0 that was mostly about leveraging robots and smart machines for maximum efficiency and high performance in manufacturing, Industry 5.0 is centred around the human impact and how latest technologies, such as IoT and Big Data, can be leveraged to empower human work and capabilities (Berg, 2022).[2]

Organisations must now align to the Business 5.0 environment. "Automation Hero coined the term 'Business 5.0.' It's the idea that automation powered by AI will drastically change company structure, business processes, and employee workflow as we know it during the coming years." (Groschupf, 2019).[3]

Industry 4.0 was techno-centric, whereas Business 5.0 is human-centric, with technology being leveraged by employees for optimal performance. It optimises human talent and ushers in the era where technological marvels enable human talent to harness their potential, for enhanced professional outcomes and beneficial business outputs. The dual purpose being, to achieve greater productivity enabled by technologies and, to ensure the well-being of employees by fostering a safe and enriching work environment. Technology is not a deterrent to peoples' employment and employability but is an enabler and accelerator for peoples' performance, with a focus on non-routine, creative, human-centric work output.

> ✓ **Business 5.0 focuses on the cyber-technology-human interface, where people and technological interactions are positive, progressive, and purposeful.**
>
> ✓ **Business 5.0 is a perceptible shift in the corporate mindset and skill sets aiming towards the optimisation of human potential through technological advancements.**
>
> ✓ **The approach to environmental factors, both internal and external, and the human perspective on managing these dynamic influences are the key differentiators in Business 5.0.**
>
> ✓ **In essence, human intelligence conceptualises, creates, empowers, and manages digital disruptions.**

⇒ Macro-level business landscape

Organisations are proactively scanning the macro-level landscape to keep abreast of the rapid digital changes taking place in Business 5.0. This involves assessing the technological trends, digital disruptions, and the extent of digitalisation in the industry. This search is not limited to intra-industry digitalisation and identifying the industry-technology convergence but is extended to industry convergence to assess the inter-industry technological adoption. To clarify:

> Industry convergence stands for new connections emerging between previously unrelated technology areas, work processes, businesses, supply chains, and even entire industry sectors. Each new connection sparks innovation and can result in significant disruption. This process of moving together can

increasingly be observed in business. Industry convergence happens as technologies, processes, businesses, and industries blend into each other to the point where they become the same. This is by no means a new phenomenon, but convergence is affected and accelerated by digitalisation (Stern, 2021a).[4]

To illustrate, "with the proliferation of novel payment platforms, cryptocurrency usage, and natural language processing, there is an opportunity to drive convergence across financial services, telecommunications, and other customer-facing industries in emerging markets" (MIT News | Massachusetts Institute of Technology, 2021).[5]

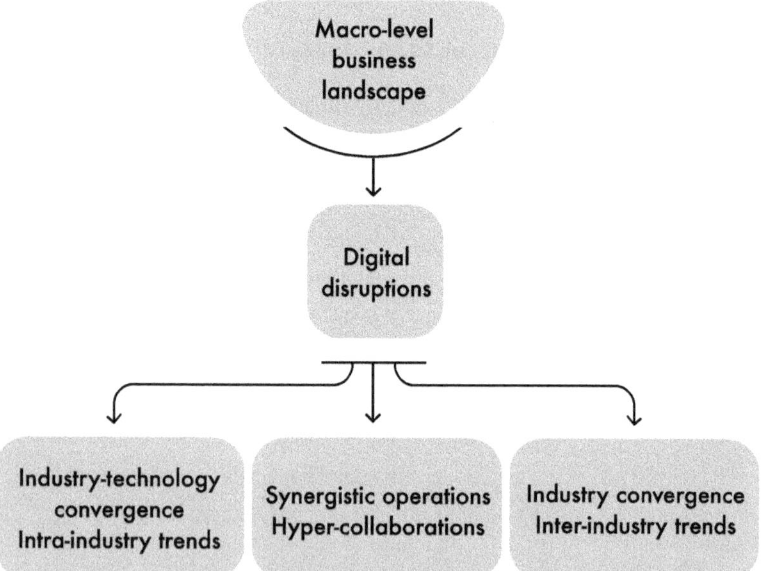

Figure 1: Macro-level business landscape

⇒ Industry-technology convergence

Intra-industry collaborations are increasing as business arrangements between and among competitors, or players in similar industries, seem more beneficial. The focus areas are the technological advancements and trends being adopted by the industry, the industry leaders' strategies, and their digital value creation related to internal and external stakeholders, leading to efficacy and synergy creation. For example, the smartphone, a device popular among all generations globally, offers the combined benefits of GPS, music, camera, social media networking, and other features leveraging disruptive technologies.

> ✓ **To survive in the established industry, organisations must match, or at the very least, follow if not surpass, the business trends and technologies that the industry leader adopts.**

⇒ Industry convergence

Industry convergence is not a new phenomenon. It has, in the past few years, been happening in some form or shape. Currently, it is happening at a fast pace due to digital disruptions, leading to technologies, processes, businesses, and industries blending with each other (Stern, 2021b).[6] For instance, the design of smart cities, as opposed to traditional cities, is digital data-driven and leverages digital disruptions. The collaborative work among architects, civil engineers, designers, fabricators, contractors, and residents includes data and workflow convergence (How—and Why—Industry Convergence Is Powering Innovation, 2021).[7] Cross-industry collaborations between and among different industrial sectors that recognise the need to work as collaborators, rather than competitors, to leverage the ecosystem and engage in partnerships and business relationships, are growing. These are global, regional, and national alliances, between and among different industries, to leverage the ecosystem.

> ✓ **Taking into cognisance, the pace and magnitude of technological and market disruptions, and acknowledging the interdependence of other industries' ecosystems, is the need of the day.**

⇒ Micro-level business landscape

The Business 5.0 organisational context necessitates a paradigm shift in the industry leaders' thinking. The cornerstones of this are the Business 5.0 strategy, leadership, and talent management. Undoubtedly, Business 5.0 is primarily related to digital transformation, which empowers employee productivity. It involves a change in systems, workflow, processes, procedures, employee work patterns and most importantly, for employees to have a digital mindset. Organisations are making informed decisions regarding the extent of digitalisation they can afford based on their business needs, financial strength, people capabilities, and the ecosystem.

Figure 2: Extent of digitalisation

1. **Digital optimisation**-All or part of the business functions and operations need to optimise their current technologies.

2. **Digital enhancement**-All or part of the business functions and operations need to enhance their current technologies.

3. **Digital transformation**-All business functions and operations need major and complete digital transformation.

02 | Business 5.0 Leadership Framework

Business 5.0 leadership framework enlists the main dimensions of effective leadership. Business 5.0 leaders, who are spearheading the transformational processes and turnaround strategies, are visualising and reimagining their organisation's sustainability in the current and future norm. They are being innovative in leveraging the ecosystem, resulting in seamless connections, leading to customer experiences and employee journeys that are beneficial. Dixit (2023) states that "now more than ever, following the shifts the workplace has seen, the importance of an effective leader and manager has grown by leaps and bounds. The current scenario demands empathetic, adaptive, and authentic leaders for their employees."[8] Business 5.0 leaders who are on the path to success exhibit seven key characteristics, as represented in the framework (Figure 3).

⇒ **Futuristic outlook**

Business 5.0 leadership is leading in uncertain times, more than ever before, and which leaders may not have experienced at such magnitude and speed. The futuristic outlook to survive in unknown territories and thrive during uncertain times is a necessity. Having a realistic vision of the way forward, and forging pathways for the corporate sector and the specific industry in which they are operating, to emerge successful in the

Business 5.0 environment, forms the guiding spirit of Business 5.0 leaders. A comprehensive and timely understanding of industry-technology convergence, and industry convergence, will support leaders in speed thinking about leveraging the ecosystem, and reaping the benefits of collaborations and alliances in Business 5.0. It gives them the awareness and alertness of stakeholder expectations and new value creation through the cyber-technology-human interface.

Figure 3: Business 5.0 leadership framework

⇒ **Business acuity**

Business 5.0 leadership is characterised by business acuity, where leaders provide visionary thinking and informed decision-making. The business acumen they have reveals the pathways and trends that organisations will encounter in the near and far future, and how to manage them efficaciously. It is the mental agility, resilience, innovation, and motivation of Business 5.0 leaders, to remain competitive and relevant in the face of fast-paced technological developments and unpredictable shifts in customer preferences, which underlie Business 5.0 decisions. Decisions that are timely and considered best in the given circumstances.

⇒ Technology savvy

The Business 5.0 leader is a digital leader equipped with knowledge of the latest, most relevant technologies and the impact these technologies have on organisations and industries. Being technology savvy will give leaders the required technological confidence and courage to determine the extent and pace of technological adoption and the relevance of digitalisation. This would instil in them a certain level of mental agility and a degree of resilience to move forward in Business 5.0. It would open their minds to the possibilities of digital value creation for meeting stakeholder expectations and giving them the trending experiences, they expect.

⇒ Stakeholder centricity

Business 5.0 leaders are inherently people-centric and have people maturity in anticipating stakeholders' requirements, understanding the multigenerational customers' expectations and patterns of employee segments. The primary and secondary stakeholders are their focus, and all efforts are directed towards this end. The endgame is stakeholder value creation and re-creation through digital content and contextualising digital output, to meet or exceed stakeholder expectations.

⇒ Ingenuity

Leaders in Business 5.0 are characterised by their ingenuity and resourcefulness. They are resourceful in networking, managing alliances, tapping human, material, financial, and physical resources, and in maintaining the reservoir for sustained development. Their ingenuity extends to all macro-level strategic decisions, micro-level business operations, systems, processes, stakeholder management, and revenue generation. They ensure sustainable development, continued business progression, and forging ahead in the Business 5.0 environs with a two-pronged approach. One is, being able to cope with disruptive technologies and market trends, and the other is, reimagining the future and producing creative and pre-emptive solutions by improvising in a timely fashion, and for the expected business outcomes.

⇒ Authenticity

Authenticity encompasses reliability, trustworthiness, honesty, courage, and confidence, which, in fact, are the salient traits of leaders. Authentic leaders inspire others and are genuine in their people management interactions and practices. They have the courage, stemming from their resilience and mental agility, to transform organisations in the Business 5.0 environment. They also have the originality to be stakeholder-centric and give stakeholders unique experiences and generate the value they expect. Employees of all generations, especially the younger generations, prefer to collaborate with authentic leaders. Authentic leaders meet the criteria for effective leadership, people management, and strategic goal achievement through their **activism, realism, and humanism.**

⇒ Mental agility

The main differentiators of Business 5.0 leaders are their strategic mindset, the mental agility with which they adapt, the resilience with which they cope and the effectiveness with which they lead change, and by being relevant at each phase of the Business 5.0 transformational process. Their ability is in foreseeing the changes, the timing of when to initiate the changes, and knowing how to manage these changes. Leading the transformation process while also being vigilant about re-transformation, its pace, and the extent of alignment with Business 5.0 will give leaders the competitive edge.

> ✓ **The Business 5.0 leader is an authentic leader, exhibiting transformational, inspirational, and value-based leadership qualities combined with a futuristic outlook and business acumen.**
>
> ✓ **They have the digital mindset to adopt technologies, manage technologies and market disruptions, with the mental agility to leverage the ecosystem, and meet stakeholder expectations through new value creation and beneficial networking.**

| 03 | Business 5.0-6 Ps Model

The Business 5.0-6 Ps model represents the main dynamics and key factors impacting organisations. The elements of the 6 Ps depict an ongoing and real-time dynamic process. The significant aspects of the 6 Ps model are continuous and are 'work in progress' at any given point in time (Figure 4).

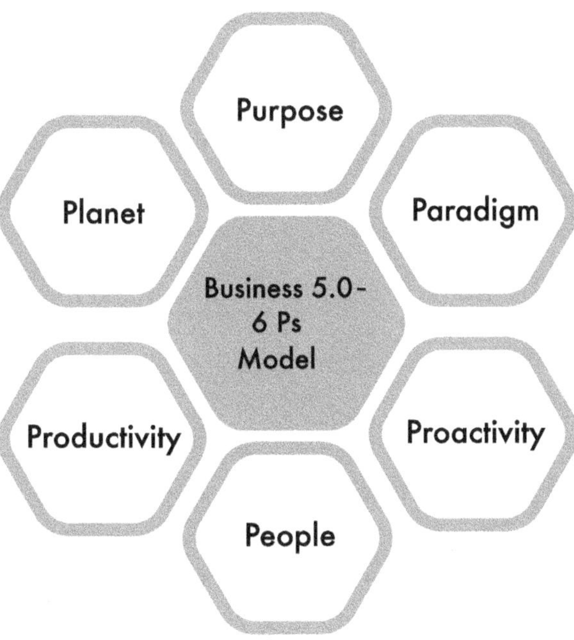

Figure 4: Business 5.0-6 Ps model

⇒ **Purpose: A business-driven mission and vision underlying stakeholder value creation.**

- The purpose of organisations is guided by visioning Business 5.0 scenarios, predicting their duration, and reimagining what the next business version and norm would be like. It involves continuous tapping of the industry, corporate, market and digital intelligence of global proportions. It implies taking into consideration how digital disruptions are shaping industrial output, and changing market segments, customer demands, and employee expectations. These ongoing developments are triggering a new norm, the duration of which is getting shorter as the new norm evolves, subsequently leading organisations to re-purpose themselves, as and when the business need arises.

- The corporate strategic planning aims to keep pace with the technological and market disruptions to thrive in Business 5.0. Planning for digital transformation resulting in product offerings that cater to the emerging needs of the markets, resulting in customer satisfaction, and aligning employee development to this transformation are the cornerstones of the Business 5.0 strategy. Strategy formulation for 'moving with' and 'moving ahead' of business disruptions is what Business 5.0 leadership should aim for.

- Leveraging the current ecosystem and envisioning the future ecosystem is a vital success indicator. Business 5.0 is marked by industry convergence, hyper-collaboration, and reaping the benefits of the existing ecosystem established by industries. It takes the form of tapping the resources made available by the ecosystem, with a sense of collaboration rather than with the objective of competition.

- Formulating a talent strategy in line with the Business 5.0 corporate strategy is crucial and paves the way for success in the Business 5.0 environment. Strategic talent planning and talent management will ensure having the right talent in organisations that will support digital transformation and propel them into the Business 5.0 environment. Talent investment is instrumental in conquering all realms and breaking all frontiers in Business 5.0.

⇒ **Paradigm: A transformative shift in people processes and techno-structures.**

- A noticeable paradigm shift is in aligning business models with the Business 5.0 vision. Business models changed from the traditional ones to the transformed models, challenging present norms and embracing Business 5.0 norms. Business models are evolving and are being reimagined due to collaborative decisions, on leveraging the ecosystem effectively. In addition, the shifting preferences of customers and changing expectations of employees make it imperative to redesign business models. Amazon, Uber, Netflix, and Airbnb were among the forerunners in this aspect.

- Organisations are restructuring hierarchical positions and resetting authority lines and limits in accordance with work patterns aligned to digital disruptions, changing markets, and shifting techno-restructuring. Traditional hierarchical structures are redundant, and current ones are blurry. The restructuring would continue to aim at an organisation design that is stakeholder friendly and suited for the Business 5.0 environment.

- Work processes, systems, and flows are being reengineered and redesigned to be in line with the Business 5.0 strategy, resulting in a market presence, revenue generation, and business continuity. The dual approach is current sustainability and future survival. Organisations must not only survive in the current environment and cater to the current markets, but must also work parallelly towards future trends and move forward, in a timely fashion, into the next norm.

- Ensuring business continuity, considering the fast-changing digital landscape and the awareness of constantly changing transformational needs, is an ongoing challenge for Business 5.0 leaders. It is essential that they assess the disruptive players and their mindsets, and forecast the disruption format and disruptive technologies. Business 5.0 leaders should be aware of the vitality of being agile in the techno-structure adaptation. They must be ever vigilant about having technological systems and business processes in place to ensure business continuity. Remodelling businesses to continuously suit the current landscape, which is characterised by a noticeably short downtime, is crucial.

- Revising people management practices and mechanisms that are employee-friendly and factor in the expectations of a multigenerational workforce cannot be more emphasised. This is considering the growing significance of employees' well-being and their ability to work with technologies, which signifies the Business 5.0 climate. It encompasses people management architecture in its entirety and, significant changes in performance management systems incorporating talent acquisition, talent development, talent management, talent compensation, talent engagement, and talent retention, to be successful in the Business 5.0 environment.

⇒ **Proactivity: Assessing current organisational culture and forecasting the business environment conducive to hosting Business 5.0.**

- Navigating changes through these dynamic and volatile times is a challenging task for even the best turnaround strategists and leaders who are well-versed in transforming organisations. Corporate changes aligned to the fast-evolving business landscape with a global understanding and outreach are the key to success in Business 5.0. Creating a culture that reflects an integrated approach to employees, and the alignment of employees with external changes, should be the top priority of managers.

- Spearheading culture immersion and encouraging employees to move out of their comfort zone and, be ready to accept and imbibe the new thinking aligned to Business 5.0 strategy, by adopting work patterns that are in line with market trends, is on the increase. Facilitating mindset change and agile thinking, by making it the default thinking mode of managers and non-managers alike, must be aimed at.

- Employees, at all levels and functions, should be aware of the changes and initiate their own adaptability to the fast-occurring changes, so they can adjust with little or no effort to the new business environs. This is especially true for adapting to the dynamic external and internal changes as a combined approach for sustainable development in Business 5.0.

⇒ **People: Leading with authenticity and managing for employee development and business sustainability.**

- Developing talent and determining talent pipelines for the near future and future talents for the next norm, forms the foundation of people management. Managing talent and people performance is a continuous effort. The way forward is to optimise employees' potential, as mutually agreed upon and in accordance with the requirements of the organisation.

- Current competency frameworks are largely based on Industry 3.0 and Industry 4.0 work outputs. Determining Business 5.0 competencies and revising current competency frameworks to capture Business 5.0 work output is essential. Competency frameworks, based on the competencies required to survive and thrive in the Business 5.0 environment, need to be finalised on a priority basis. This would then become the point of departure, for modifying all other people management practices and their interconnectivity.

- Organisations, currently, have four generations working with them [Baby Boomers, Generation X, Millennials, and Generation Z]. The major game changers are younger generations whose compensation expectations are significantly different from those that of the earlier generations. Customising reward systems that meet the expectations of the multiculturally diverse employee groups of various generations, is a vital factor in employee engagement and employee retention.

- Organisations need to work towards adopting hybrid work patterns and people management practices. People management practices need to significantly change. People managers and people management advisers must modify people management practices and formulate policies for the next generations. This necessitates a different people management perspective that meets the differing expectations of the diverse employee groups.

⇒ **Productivity: New skilling acquired through continuous learning and development.**

- Identifying competency gaps and determining employees' areas of development as relevant for Business 5.0 will support the employee learning and development plans and learning journeys. Estimating the currency of talent pipelines and, the need to revitalise talent pipelines with the latest and the next norm talent, is becoming a major part of the learning and development function.

- Mental agility, resilience, business continuity, and sustainable development, the key ingredients for thriving in Business 5.0, become a reality through new skilling initiatives. Talent life cycles are becoming shorter as employees progress into the next norm. Right skilling characterises the learning and development function. The return on investment in new skilling will be realised when organisations prioritise employees' continuous learning and put employees' new skilling at the forefront. They also need to create a learning environment that is conducive to employees' new skilling and continuously facilitates their right skilling.

- The talent life cycle stages of employees need to be analysed, and the right skilling development plans should be established to bridge the reskilling and upskilling gaps. It requires reskilling employees with new skill sets and mindsets for evolving future jobs and, upskilling employees with improved skill sets and mindsets to be productive and relevant in the current workplace scenarios. Reskilled and upskilled employees will wade successfully in the industry convergence.

- Persevering, wading through the transformation process, and emerging successful is imperative for every employee in the organisation. This eventually will lead to the expected organisational outcomes in Business 5.0. Creating a learning culture where employees proactively seek development in areas that interest them, appeal to their career progression, and which is useful for the organisation in realising its corporate strategy.

⇒ **Planet: Deliver environmental, social, and governance (ESG) initiatives through a judicious mix of technology blend and human values to usher in an ethical organisational governance, social betterment, and ecological balance.**

- The crises that planet Earth is facing are primarily about environmental pollution, leading to an ecological imbalance. The dire need is to make a concentrated effort on all fronts, by all walks of people in every community, locally, regionally, and globally, to reduce environmental pollution and uphold the environmental sanctity of planet Earth.

Specifically, organisations are now, more than ever before, bound by ESG standards, as it has become a worldwide movement and the focus of business leaders. It is now mandated and regulated by authorities for organisations to take responsibility and accountability for environmental issues and the communities in which they operate (Conmy, n.d.).[9]

- From a social point of view, the contribution of organisations to human and societal welfare is significant. Working for the upliftment of humankind and underprivileged sections of people exhibits their commitment and values towards social causes and social betterment.

- Governance of organisations with ethical principles embedded in the rules, regulations, procedures, control mechanisms, processes, overall leadership, and management practices, leads to ethical governance on all fronts.

- Employees are more likely to prefer organisations that are committed to sustainable development goals and are translating these goals into action and initiatives, which are bearing the right results. They are likely to associate and be more engaged with such organisations. Customer groups are people drawn from the same generations as those of the employee groups, having a similar level of consciousness and mindfulness of the sellers' commitment to achieving ESG goals.

- ESG goals and their attainment function as a beacon and are an important decision-making criterion for investment and business collaboration in Business 5.0. The essence of it is the responsibility and accountability taken by organisations in achieving them.

According to Thygesen (2019), "ESG causes can be strong environment standards, such as sustainable natural materials, water conservation and CO2 reductions. Or they can be advancing social issues, such as diversity in workforce and leadership, human rights, or poverty reduction. Or they can revolve around ethical corporate governance measures, such as anti-corruption and capped executive compensation."[10] Andrews (2023) emphasises that "environmental, social and governance (ESG) considerations may have a significant impact on an organization's reputation and ability to attract both employees and customers."[11]

✓ **Business 5.0-6 Ps model is an all-pervasive model for forward-thinking organisations that want to be future-ready.**

04 | Business 5.0 Standpoints

Business 5.0 content and context determine the Business 5.0 capabilities, which in turn are linked to employee capabilities. The capabilities required for sustainable development in Business 5.0 should manifest in each employee's capabilities.

Figure 5: Employee capabilities

⇒ Business 5.0 mindset and skill sets

Employee capabilities are an outcome of the combination of the Business 5.0 mindset and the Business 5.0 skill sets. The Business 5.0 mindset is an awareness and acceptance of the rapid changes occurring due to disruptive technologies, industry convergence, and people empowerment. The superseding factor is that technological advancements and human capabilities lead to higher productivity. Business 5.0 'ready' employees tend to continue the cyber-technology-human journey, which is unfolding, in a proactive and progressive manner. In Business 5.0, employees need to be continuously new skilled to reap the benefits of the cyber-technology-human efficacy.

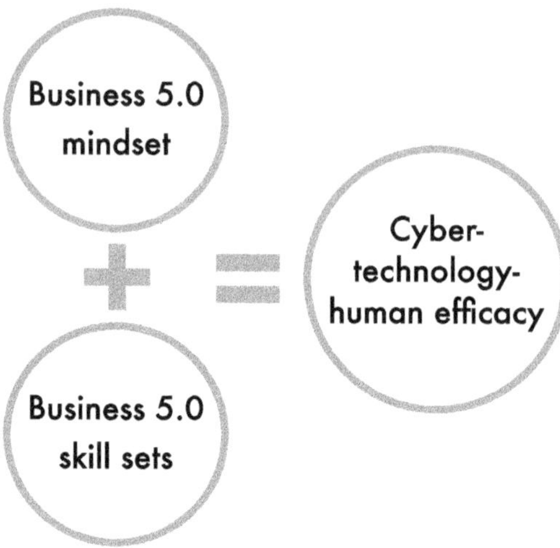

Figure 6: Business 5.0 efficacy

New skilling is the need of the day. "The new world of work requires people to continuously hone their skills to stay relevant and improve their employability. The term new skilling represents all types of continuous learning to help build high-demand skills, whether an individual is trying to upskill current capabilities, or needs complete reskilling to build entirely new capabilities" (Cornerstone, n.d.).[12]

Reskilling, in general, is focused on employees being promoted, assigning them new projects, and providing them with opportunities for vertical, horizontal, cross-functional, and new function career pathways. It encompasses equipping employees with the required mindset and skill sets for projected job assignments and career pathways.

Upskilling includes the training and development initiatives that organisations offer their employees on an ongoing basis, to meet the standards of work in terms of quantity and quality. They need to improve themselves by acquiring the right skill sets to do better in their current jobs, which would lead to job enrichment and next-level jobs in the same career pathway or a different one, as deemed suitable by the organisation (TalentGuard, 2019).[13]

Key skill sets and mindset dimensions to focus on, for success in the Business 5.0 environment, are given in Figure 7.

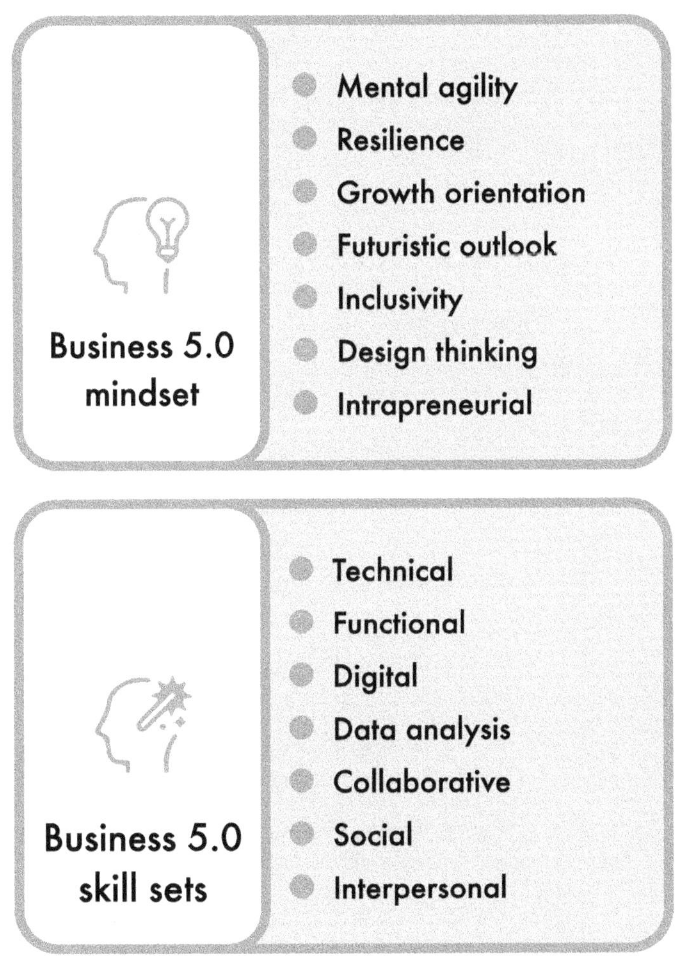

Figure 7: Business 5.0 mindset and skill sets.

⇨ **Business 5.0 mindset and skill sets matrix**

The Business 5.0 mindset and skill sets matrix (Figure 8) indicates combinations of levels of mindset and skill sets prevalent among employees. New skilling of leaders and facilitating the new skilling of employees is a step in the right direction in the Business 5.0 environment. Keeping an open mind to learn and to think in accordance with the requirements of Business 5.0, will propel organisations into the future, with the capabilities and confidence to compete in Business 5.0 markets.

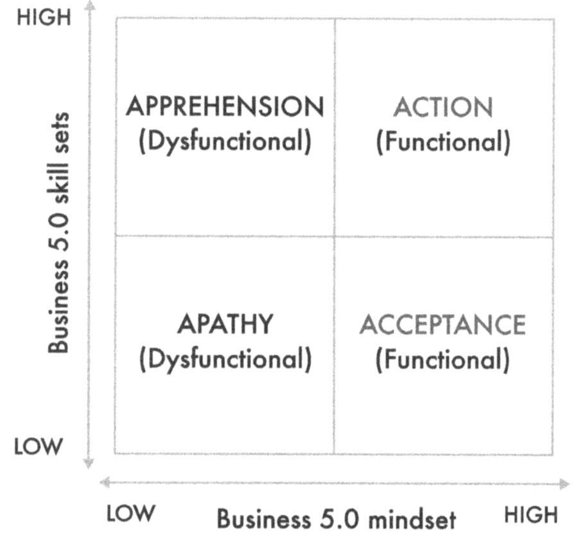

Figure 8: Business 5.0 mindset and skill sets matrix.

Functional stages
Acceptance: High level of Business 5.0 mindset and low level of Business 5.0 skill sets.
Employees who have the right mindset are aware of the need to acquire the skill sets to survive and thrive in the Business 5.0 environment. They find it easy to learn new skills and adapt to the Business 5.0 requirements. Such employees are in the acceptance stage, which is functional and gives them the momentum to proactively acquire relevant skill sets and right skill themselves to face the challenges ahead.
Action: High level of Business 5.0 mindset and high level of Business 5.0 skill sets.
Business 5.0 is, in fact, an action-oriented set-up. Employees with the right mindset and skill sets, and who are dealing with the changes occurring through a proactive and futuristic approach are the best-fit employees, contributing to the functionality that organisations are aiming for. This high level of mindset and skill sets gives them the motivation and competitive edge one expects in the ever-changing Business 5.0 environment.

Dysfunctional stages
Apathy: Low level of Business 5.0 mindset and low level of Business 5.0 skill sets.
As indicated in the Business 5.0 mindset and skill sets matrix, employees with a low level of Business 5.0 mindset and skill sets are evidently lagging and are in a state of apathy. This dysfunctional stage requires **radical shake-up** and **employee wake-up** measures to ensure that the criticality of business survival is realised by employees. If such apathy continues unchecked, organisations may slowly be phased out of the business, and the most adversely affected group would be the employees themselves, through loss of employment.

> **Apprehension: Low level of Business 5.0 mindset and high level of Business 5.0 skill sets.**
>
> The apprehension stage is the other dysfunctional stage, in which employees are equipped with the right skill sets but are not motivated enough to use them effectively. They need to have the right mindset to move ahead. This may be made possible, by impressing upon them the need to gain the right thinking, and motivating them to adapt to the changes, and implementing them effectively. This stage requires interventions like counselling, empathy mapping, and human perspectives to encourage employees to actively participate in the digital transformation process and adapt to the Business 5.0 environment.

Continuous monitoring and a concentrated effort is required on part of the Business 5.0 leaders to identify employees belonging to each mindset and skill sets stage. They need to formulate human-related interactions and interventions like coaching, mentoring, counselling, empathy mapping, and psychological safety for employees to overcome the fear and resistance emanating from the **apathy** and **apprehension** stages. They need to redirect the energies of employee groups who are in the **acceptance** and **action** stages into the learning and development area, through career discussions and career mapping.

Employee groups may not necessarily remain at the same stages they are in; they may move from a required functional stage [acceptance and action] to a dysfunctional stage [apathy and apprehension], and vice versa. This requires a highly dynamic monitoring process that reflects and captures external changes and digital disruptions and, identifies the internal redesign and remodelling that is appropriate. This aids in guiding employees to remain in the functional stages or move to the functional stages.

At no stage can the leadership be lax, as the time lag between onboarding employees, right skilling them, and implementing the changes, is only a temporary phase in Business 5.0. Changes are looming large on organisations, making all previous efforts quickly redundant. Adapting to changes at the right time to capture the market, being in line with industry trends, and being on the lookout for the next level of transformation, should be embedded in the thinking patterns of employees and leaders in Business 5.0. Being slack or investing time and perpetuating the wrong mindset and skill sets, could cost organisations heavily in terms of market loss, and employee morale, and may even threaten their very existence.

✓ **Resistance to change is a luxury one cannot afford in the Business 5.0 environment.**

⇒ **Business 5.0 learning model**

The conscious competence learning model, as applicable to Business 5.0, comprises four stages.[1] These four stages are a mix of these two factors - **conscious** and **competence**:

"Conscious – how aware we are of what we know or what we can do.

---

[1] The Conscious Competence Learning Model was first described by Management Trainer Martin Broadwell in 1969. Noel Burch then developed the Conscious Competence Ladder in the 1970s while working at Gordon Training. Source: https://learning-ninja.com/conscious-competence-model-or-4-stages-of-learning/ [Accessed 12 Sep. 2023]

Competence – whether we have the skills to do the things we need to do.

1. Unconscious Incompetence Stage – you do not know what you do not know.

2. Conscious Incompetence Stage – you know what you don't know.

3. Conscious Competence Stage – you know that you can do it now.

4. Unconscious Competence Stage – you can do it without thinking about it" (www.revolutionlearning.co.uk, n.d.).[14]

The Business 5.0 learning model (Figure 9) adapted from the conscious competence learning model indicates that the learning stages have a limited life and are iterative. As soon as organisations and employees have awareness of the stage they are in, that stage would have passed, making way for the next stage.

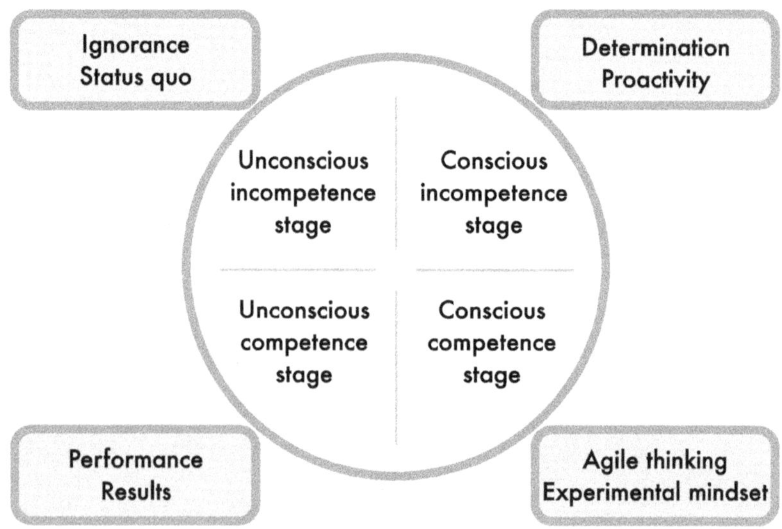

Figure 9: Business 5.0 learning model

Unconscious incompetence stage

This is a perennial stage leading organisations to the threshold of the next norm. A stage in which organisations **do not know what they do not know,** about where the technologies, customer patterns, and employee journeys would take them, how they would evolve, and the likely business disruptions that may continue to occur. This stage can be overcome by being alert to the changes occurring, being resourceful in accessing multi-source information and benchmarking globally. Undoubtedly, it is an ongoing process.

Conscious incompetence stage

In this stage, organisations are aware of the magnitude of changes in Business 5.0 and their impact, as well as one's competence and ability to cope with these rapid changes. Organisations and large sections of employee groups may either be ignorant of the disruptions or, may be aware of the disruptions but may not be cognisant of the impact of such disruptions, or may be aware of the impact but not know how to manage the changes and implement systems for success in Business 5.0. A stage in which employees are fully aware of their level of competence and the extent to which they can cope with, and face the challenges posed by Business 5.0. This is a crucial stage in which reskilling and upskilling decisions are taken and new skilling initiatives are rolled out. Business 5.0 decisions emanate from this phase, thereby propelling organisations to the 'conscious competence' stage.

Conscious competence stage

This is a stage where new skilled employees are managing the changes, catering to customer expectations, aligning with market trends, and gaining valuable knowledge and expertise in understanding how the business will grow and move forward. Employees are aligned to Business 5.0 and, are fully aware of the short-lived situation and the short-term continuity of the trends they are aware of and practices they became familiar with.

Unconscious competence stage

The challenge is, that, this stage is fleeting, as the technological and market disruptions occurring may impact employees' competence. Organisations should tap the expertise and optimise the productivity of employees. This stage supports in achieving the strategic goals and, gaining a financial and marketing base that paves the way for the future. This stage poses a major transformation on the part of employees and organisations. It very likely transports them to the 'unconscious incompetence' stage, due to the latest disruptions overwhelming Business 5.0, where they, once again, **do not know what they do not know**, instead of taking them to the next stage, which is the 'conscious unconscious competence' stage.

Conscious unconscious competence stage

The 'conscious unconscious competence stage' is a very temporary and elusive state to achieve in the Business 5.0 environment and the digital disruption era. Some organisations may not even reach this stage. It is generally referred to as a stage in which employees are aware of their competence, can reflect on their expertise and performance, and are able to assess, analyse their competence and support others in their learning.

> ✓ **The Business 5.0 journey and onwards is an infinite learning loop. The learning loop is set on a fast speed mode and is moving at a fast pace on the learning model and journey.**

⇒ Business 5.0 roadmap

In Business 5.0, organisations are being redesigned to factor in the cyber-technology-human interface, the trending customer experiences, and modified employee journeys. According to Carucci and Sharpell (2022), the most common misstep is the failure to redesign organisations. It is not just the strategy that will set organisations' differentiators, but organisational capabilities that will give them the competitive edge.[15] Redesigning organisations with new business capabilities is initiated through reskilling and upskilling employees. The techno-processes and techno-structures need revamping. The systems flow, workflow, and time flow need to be aligned to the trending customer experiences and modified employee journeys, resulting in unique and differentiated cyber-technology-stakeholder interfaces (Figure 10).

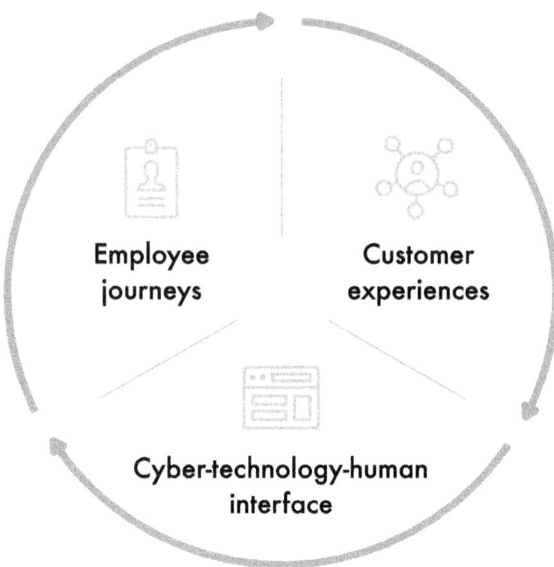

Figure 10: Organisation design

Customer experiences need to be segmented and customised, as product offerings in Business 5.0 are varied, numerous, and innovative. Keeping in line, if not ahead of other collaborators in the market, is necessary for survival. Providing the experiences expected by customers is the unified and concentrated effort of employee groups. Employee journeys need to be synchronised for efficacy in the Business 5.0 environment. Organisations need to be ahead of collaborators, in offering better employee journeys and customer experiences, as this forms the basis for thriving and moving towards the turn ahead.

A simplistic Business 5.0 roadmap is exhibited in Figure 11 and detailed in Table 1.

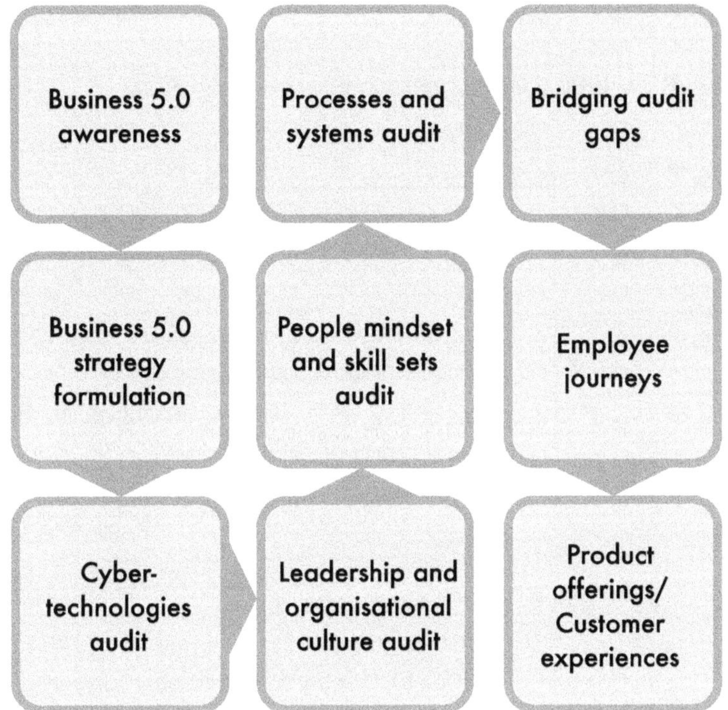

Figure 11: Business 5.0 roadmap

⇒ Business 5.0 focus areas and actions

The focus areas and the actions to be taken by organisations aligned to the Business 5.0 roadmap are given in Table 1.

Table 1: Business 5.0 roadmap-Focus areas and actions

Focus Area	Action
Business 5.0 awareness	• Tap and seek information on Business 5.0, current technological disruptions, and market trends. • Identify resources to adapt to the transformed Business 5.0 landscape. • Benchmark with industry changes, trends, and practices of collaborators. • Seek feedback, input, and ideas from internal and external stakeholders impacting the business. • Actively monitor the business environment and emerging trends. • Conduct Business 5.0 awareness sessions for Board members, C-suite executives, managers, and non-managers.
Business 5.0 strategy formulation	• Formulate Business 5.0 strategy considering the business landscape and the changes likely to occur. • Build in strategic agility for a futuristic approach. • Communicate the Business 5.0 strategy in understandable terms to all stakeholders.

Focus Area	Action
Cyber-technologies audit	• Conduct an audit of current and emerging technologies required to achieve the Business 5.0 strategy. • Identify the gaps and the level of technological advancements to be adopted for the transformation process to be successful. • Determine the best blend of technologies with the option to upgrade to the next level of advancement.
Leadership and organisational culture audit	• Assess the prevailing organisational culture and leadership philosophy, their styles, values, and vision. • Gauge if the leadership can provide the guidance and direction, to take the organisation forward, for it to be successful in the Business 5.0 environment.
People mindset and skill sets audit	• Assess the current mindset and existing skill sets of employees on an individual basis, team level, department level, and organisation level. • Develop reskilling and upskilling programmes aligned to the Business 5.0 new skilling strategy.
Processes and systems audit	• Audit established systems and current processes to determine the reengineering, remodelling, and redesign suitable for Business 5.0. • Finalise the redesign of processes, systems, structures, and mechanisms appropriate for technological usage, interface, and advancement in Business 5.0.

Focus Area	Action
Bridging audit gaps	• Plan and finalise initiatives and interventions, to bridge the identified audit gaps. • Implement the bridging interventions, to counter and overcome the challenges in Business 5.0 • Create the right culture and environment conducive to thrive in the Business 5.0 environment.
Employee journeys	• Design people management policies and practices, to support employees' onboarding and initiation into the Business 5.0 environment. • Plan employee journeys that are ideal for offering the customer experiences, and achieving the strategic goals, as envisioned.
Product offerings/ Customer experiences	• Plan to offer appropriate product offerings and trending customer experiences, on par with collaborators and market leaders, in the Business 5.0 arena.

> ✓ **Business 5.0 roadmap is a dynamic strategic tool, as the milestones and timelines keep changing due to digital disruptions and market trends.**

PART 2 | PEOPLE MANAGEMENT

Chapters

5   People Engagement 55

6   People Enablement 85

7   People Management Practices 93

05 | People Engagement

People management is the underlying 'make' or 'break' feature in Business 5.0., as it is essentially an integrated work approach where employees access technologies for a productive cyber-technology interface. Focusing on the different age generations, providing an integrated employee value proposition [IEVP], and contributing to the diversity, equity, inclusion, and belonging [DEIB] culture, employee well-being and mental health, are gaining momentum in Business 5.0. In addition, the relevance of global citizenship, people analytics, and knowledge management are trending. The aim of people management in Business 5.0 is to maximise employee engagement and employee retention, by focusing more on work-life fit rather than work-life balance practices, and by minimising quiet quitting and loud quitting.

⇒ Multigenerational workforce

People management in the Business 5.0 environment is an ongoing review of the multigenerational workforce. Currently, organisations have four generations working with them [in 2023], with the entry of the fifth generation (Generation Alpha) within a few years. The categorisation[16] of these five generations is given in Figure 12.

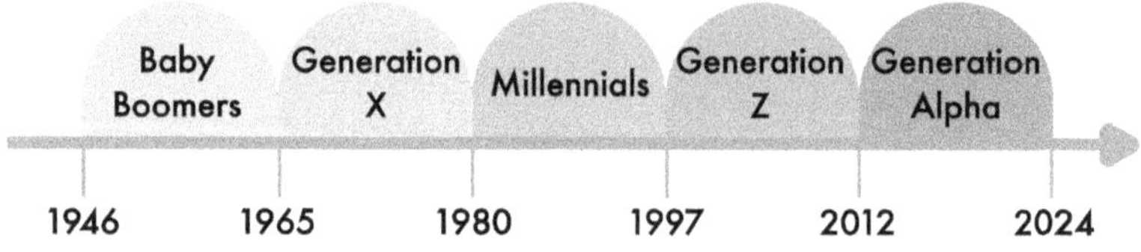

Figure 12: Five generations categorisation

The technological familiarity and capabilities of people led to categorising different generations of people as 'digital natives' and 'digital immigrants' (coined by Marc Prensky in 2001).[2] Millennials, Generation Z, and Generation Alpha who grew up in the information age, are referred to as the 'digital natives.' Generation X, Baby Boomers and earlier generations are referred to as the 'digital immigrants' (Hasa, 2022).[17] The main characteristics of 'digital natives' are that they are "tech-savvy, ethnically diverse and aware, good at online social interactions, prefer personalised learning, and readily embrace metaverse devices and experiences" (Amuno, 2018).[18] "Generation Z's identity has been shaped by the digital age, climate anxiety, a shifting financial landscape, and COVID-19" (McKinsey, 2023).[19]

People managers are at the crossroads of this generation flow, especially those managers who belong to Generation X and 'older' Millennial categories. People managers of these generations learnt and developed skill sets, mindsets, systems, processes, work patterns, and people management styles, under the guidance of people managers who belong to the Baby Boomers and 'older' Generation X categories.

[2.] Digital Natives, Digital Immigrants By Marc Prensky From On the Horizon (MCB University Press, Vol. 9 No. 5, October 2001) © 2001 Marc Prensky

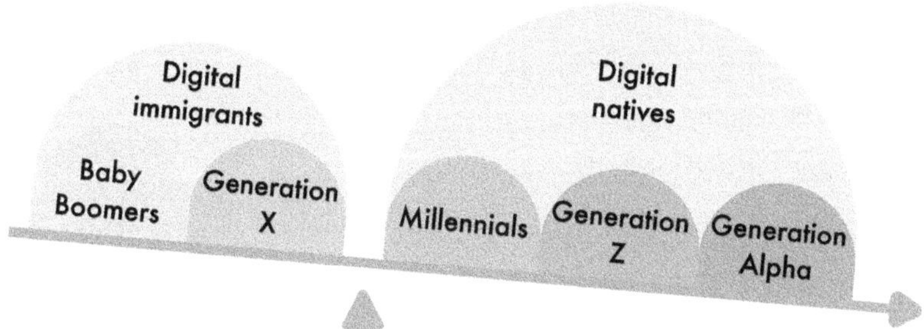

Figure 13: Digital immigrants and digital natives

People managers who are in their thirties [age in 2023] have on an average, three or more decades of corporate life ahead of them. They must now manage the younger generations effectively. At this juncture, they need to shed their earlier thinking and practices, unlearn unhelpful work patterns, and relearn how to be successful as an employee and as a people manager, in the stream of the multigenerational workforce. They must revitalise their people management practices to meet the expectations of Generation Z and Generation Alpha and be easily accepted by them.

Though research and available literature has established standards and common characteristics of different generations, these standards and characteristics are only descriptive and predictive. The prescription for each generation depends on the country of their origin and/or in which they are living, the geopolitical backdrop, sociocultural fabric, family upbringing, financial background, educational record, lifestyle choices, and individual preferences. These factors play a significant role in defining the characteristics of each generation, their work culture, and their career expectations. Though a broad categorisation is the starting point in understanding different generations in general, people managers need to conduct specific studies and focused assessments, locally and regionally, to assimilate the psychographics, requirements, and expectations of each generation and the environs which shaped them.

This transforms the people management function, necessitating revamping the recruitment strategies, identifying different sourcing methods, employing a combination of selection methods, and onboarding programmes that are suitable for the younger generations. The future is, most definitely, about competitive employer branding, with the next generations more likely to choose to work with organisations that are purpose driven, offer an IEVP, have widespread employee well-being programmes, work-life fit practices, DEIB policies, ESG initiatives, and value-based leadership.

> ✓ **The future is for the digital leader and not the digital laggard.**

⇒ **Integrated employee value proposition [IEVP]**

The employer philosophy and the role of people managers are evolving. In the wake of this multigenerational workforce that organisations are characterised by, employers must put an innovative effort into enhancing their employee value proposition [EVP]. An employee value proposition is:

> The unique value you offer as an employer to your employees in return for their skills, experience, and commitment to your company. This includes components like salary, benefits, rewards, career develop-

ment, and work-life balance, as well as your values, mission, social purpose, and organizational culture. Essentially, your EVP aims to identify and communicate all the unique benefits and experiences that employees can expect from choosing to work for your organization. It also communicates why your company is the right place for the employees who thrive there and helps you attract the right people who align with your unique offering (Verlinden, n.d.).[20]

EVP encompasses the value that organisations are offering to their employees at each stage of the employee life cycle, from the pre-hiring stage to the post-separation stage: spread over resourcing, placement, learning and development, performance management, compensation and benefits, rewards and recognition, succession planning, and separation. Organisations need to align their EVP with different generations and customise them based on the talent segment of employees within the given generation. The job market is metamorphosing into different talent segments and differing generational subgroups. Different offerings and employee value propositions catering to these segments and subgroups need to be identified and defined by organisations. The value proposition is a generation wise, segment-based offering aimed at segment fit career-seekers, extending to individual preferences through work-life fit practices, which encourage employees to engage and stay in the organisation. This involves, determining the IEVP applicable to an age-related generation, incorporating components catering to specific talent segments, and including customised propositions appealing to individuals.

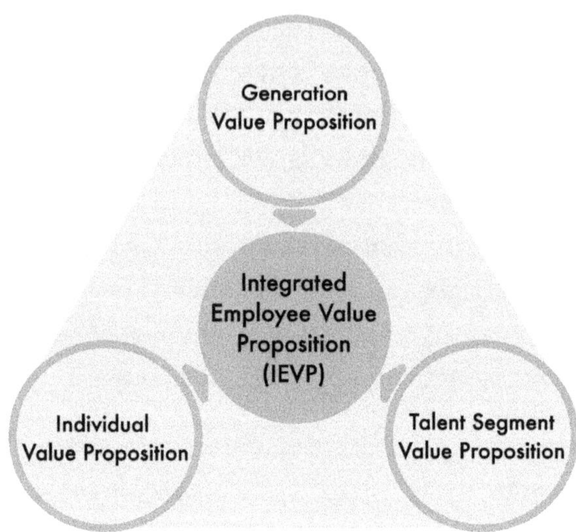

Figure 14: Integrated Employee Value Proposition [IEVP]

Individuals, irrespective of the segment or generation they belong to, give equal importance to the economic contract as much as the psychological contract.[3] The economic contract extends to having a fair and equity-based total reward system and majorly focuses on career growth and development. The psychological contract rests heavily on the sense of belonging, well-being, and global identity. People managers need to identify and monitor all those components and factors that contribute to strengthening the economic contract and psychological contract, alike. This involves a fair exchange for the professionalism with which employees work for the

---

[3.] Psychological contract-An unwritten set of expectations and obligations between the employer and employee, where the promises and obligations as expected are met.

benefit of the organisation. The major challenge facing people managers is in understanding the generational subgroup requirements, talent segment composition, and their expectations. The end goal is to identify practices that would appeal to, attract, and retain these generational subgroups and talent segments, with the flexibility to customise them for individuals as required.

> ✓ **Integrated employee value proposition [IEVP] reflects a judicious combination of: common policies for age-related generations, variation in policies for different talent segments, and flexibility in policies for individuals.**

⇒ **Diversity, equity, inclusion and belonging [DEIB]**

Diversity and inclusion have been the focus areas of the corporate world. Organisations were proactively ushering in diversity and inclusion through affirmative actions, setting hard and soft quotas to fill in positions with people from the under-represented/unrepresented groups to make the workforce inclusive. This did not lead to the expected outcomes. Disparity and discrimination are still rampant. The diversity and inclusion policies and practices created an environment for equity, where employees of all diverse groups are treated on an equitable basis and have a sense of belonging. This gave rise to the DEIB culture.

According to Govindaraju (2021), "DEIB efforts, though disparate, have increasingly become woven into organizational policies and practices to reflect the composition of society."[21] "Diversity—through the lenses of race, ethnicity, ability, gender, sexual orientation, neurodiversity, and beyond—can help to strengthen organizations, as studies have shown time and again" (McKinsey & Company, 2022).[22] An important development which is of great interest to people management professionals is that of neurodiversity, in addition to biodiversity. The term neurodiversity is being used:

> To represent a fast-growing sub-category of organisational diversity and inclusion that seeks to embrace and maximise the talents of people who think differently. Autism, dyslexia, dyspraxia, ADHD (attention deficit hyperactivity disorder) and more – for so long pathologised as medical conditions to be mitigated, and even cured – are now seen as natural forms of human neurocognitive variation. What have been termed the 'flip side' strengths of neurodivergent individuals – from problem-solving, to creative insights and visual spatial thinking – are belatedly being recognised (CIPD, 2018a).[23]

Kennedy (2023) states that "supporting neurodiverse employees with sensory processing needs is essential for creating an inclusive workplace. By creating a sensory-friendly environment, offering flexible work arrangements, educating managers and co-workers, and creating a sensory processing plan for each employee, employers can create an environment where all employees can thrive."[24] This also validates that sensory processing ability is a key skill identified by the World Economic Forum in their 'Future of Jobs 2023' report (given in Table 6). Sensory processing ability is now becoming a mainstream training trend to create a work culture conducive for neurodiverse employees to make them feel safe and for them to have a sense of belonging in organisations.

Organisations are investing resources to have a diverse workforce and ensure inclusivity, as this is a key contributor to employee well-being. Inclusivity inherent in policies, embedded in the work culture, and as an integral part of organisational ethos will give that sense of belonging and equity, which employees expect from organisations. The formula for success lies in effective leadership, and progressive people management practices that result in a fair, equitable, and non-discriminatory professional exchange with employees. On the personal front, it manifests as diversity in all forms and inclusivity at all levels, resulting in a sense of belonging and psychological safety for employees.

"Belonging at work adds to the DEI equation. If we put our philosophical hat on for a second, we could say that, on the one hand, it is about "longing to be." On the other hand, it is about "being for long," representing an affective and a temporal dimension. Belonging in the workplace brings a shift towards psychological safety and real inclusion" (Verlinden, 2022).[25] Being conscious of the 'unconscious bias' also referred to as implicit bias, characterises employee behaviour nowadays. It is stated that:

Both unconscious and explicit bias involve judging others based on our assumptions rather than objective facts. However, the two are quite different. Unconscious bias occurs when we have an inclination for or against a person or group that emerges automatically.

Explicit bias includes positive or negative attitudes that we are fully aware of and openly express. These attitudes form part of our worldview. Despite their differences, unconscious bias can be just as problematic as explicit bias. Both can lead to discriminatory behavior (Nikolopoulou, 2023).[26]

Formulating inherently bias free, equity-based work systems and people management mechanisms is the main purpose of this movement. This is, indeed, a movement and not just an initiative, because employee groups carry generational biases and prejudices into the workplace. Eradicating societal evils emanating from differences based on class, income, religion, and ethnicity, which are ingrained in communities and became a part of the employees' upbringing, and thereby formed their thinking process about equity. In addition, unethical people management practices, managers, and employee groups indulging in discriminatory behaviour, both covert and overt, may not be firmly dealt with in organisations. Senior managers may be ignoring these corporate atrocities or are oblivious to the anti-social and anti-human treatment being meted out to the victims.

There are two groups of employees coming from communities riddled with these evils, one group constituting the victims who are at the receiving end of this discrimination, and the other group comprising the perpetrators who have difficulty in controlling their discriminatory behaviour and are non-compliant with systems mitigating these behaviours. The behavioural choices made by these two groups must be identified, captured, and addressed appropriately. The behavioural choices negating the DEIB culture on part of the managers, employee groups, and individuals should be a key dimension in their performance evaluation. A behavioural modification process, performance improvement plan, and mindset change intervention should be put in place, for shaping employees' behaviour to comply with, and contribute to the DEIB culture.

The multigenerational workforce would like to see DEIB woven into the sociocultural and personal fabric of the organisation. It should be applied within the professional work requirements, which support valid criteria and business bona fide requirements that permit differentiation of employees based on meritocracy, but not discrimination based on personal biases and social prejudices.

Imbibing the spirit of equity and developing 'justice sensitivity' is a phenomenon common to humankind and can be noticed even in children. "Justice sensitivity is the tendency to notice and identify wrong-doing and injustice and have intense cognitive, emotional, and behavioural reactions to that injustice. People who are justice sensitive tend to notice injustice more often than others, they tend to ruminate longer and more intensely on that injustice, and they feel a stronger need to restore justice" (Masters, 2022).[27]

Justice sensitive employees tend to notice anomalies, unfairness, discrimination, unethical behaviour, and unprofessional practices and sense them instantly. They act or speak about it with the intention of minimising the impact of these injustices, if not eliminating them. Their activism spreads quickly, as other employees who may have noticed the injustices but preferred not to challenge them, may join the activism. An organisational culture where employee voice is recognised and encouraged, instead of suppressed and punished, would go a long way in creating the desired DEIB culture. "Employee voice is often defined as giving people opportunities to express ideas, concerns, and perspectives with authenticity and without fear of social or workplace consequences. That means employees have the ability to influence decisions at work through their feedback" (Wong, 2020).[28] Having influence means business leaders act based on dialogue with employees. Action could represent a new way of completing work, innovative work processes, improving culture, or resolving problem areas in the organisation.

This implies that employees should speak up for the right reasons, in the right manner, at the right time, and in the right place. Organisations must encourage a two-way communication and be open to feedback. Managers should be professional in their approach to constructive feedback. Employees who are speaking about things that matter may be doing so because they are interested in staying in the organisation and, want to make it a professional environment for their well-being and that of their colleagues.

> ✓ **There should be no discrimination against employees due to any disparity, but only differentiation of employees based on job fit and talent optimisation.**

⇒ Employee well-being and mental health

Employee well-being and mental health are at the forefront of organisations' strategies. This is a hot button topic and a priority area globally, in communities and organisations. Employee well-being denotes employees being in a state of wellness, having a sense of safety, a feeling of accomplishment, the knowledge of being accepted, and an awareness of being cared for and taken care of. It is one, or a combination of all these factors, that goes into strengthening individual psychological safety and making employee well-being a robust area. It is stated that:

> Investing in employee wellbeing can lead to increased resilience, better employee engagement, reduced sickness absence and higher performance and productivity. However, wellbeing initiatives often fall short of their potential because they stand alone, isolated from the everyday business. To gain real benefit, employee wellbeing priorities must be integrated throughout an organisation, embedded in its culture, leadership, and people management (CIPD, 2023a).[29]

Organisations are focussing on dimensions relevant to and impacting employee well-being, such as physical, social, intellectual, financial, occupational, emotional, environmental, and spiritual (GoodTherapy.org, 2016).[30] "There's no 'one-size-fits-all' approach to designing a health and wellbeing strategy; its content should be based on the unique needs and characteristics of the organisation and its workforce" (CIPD, 2023b).[31] Moving forward, employee well-being dimensions may remain the same, but the content and context that comprise them will change to encapsulate the problems, issues, concerns, and frustrations which people may face, especially the younger generations. "In its 2021 Global Risks Report, the World Economic Forum ranks 'youth disillusionment' as the eighth of ten immediate risks. Findings include deteriorating mental health since the start of the pandemic, leaving 80% of young people worldwide vulnerable to depression, anxiety, and disappointment" (Masterson, 2022).[32] Mental health:

> Is a state of mental well-being that enables people to cope with the stresses of life, realize their abilities, learn well, and work well, and contribute to their community. It is an integral component of health and well-being that underpins our individual and collective abilities to make decisions, build relationships and shape the world we live in. Mental health is a basic human right. And it is crucial to personal, community and socio-economic development (World Health Organization (WHO), 2022).[33]

The eight major dimensions contributing to employee well-being are enumerated in Table 2.

Table 2: Eight dimensions of employee well-being

1. Physical wellness
"Physical wellness consists of recognizing the need for physical activity, healthy foods, and sleep, as well as preventing illness and injury or managing chronic health conditions" (www.northwestern. edu, n.d.).[34] Physical wellness is taking the shape of healthy eating, gymnasium visits, physical workouts, and maintaining a healthy body. The physical stress of employees, in the form of digital fatigue, excessive screen time, blurriness in vision, and long hours of sedentary work, is being addressed now.
2. Emotional wellness
According to Resnick (2021), "emotional wellness, which is also known as emotional health or emotional wellbeing, is a person's ability to handle their emotions and the varied experiences they encounter in life."[35] Emotional wellness manifests in having an emotional balance in dealing with personal challenges and social relationships. It requires gaining awareness and acceptance of shortcomings in one's behavioural patterns and interactions and, working on them for better personal and social outcomes. Recognising one's emotional traits and emotional equilibrium and managing them intelligently are becoming relevant.
3. Intellectual wellness
"Intellectual wellness refers to active participation in scholastic, cultural, and community activities. It is important to gain and maintain intellectual wellness because it expands knowledge and skills to live a stimulating, successful life. To improve intellectual wellness, it is important to value creativity, curiosity, and lifelong learning" (Illinois State University, 2016).[36] Intellectual wellness lies in acquiring jobs/portfolios, which the employee favours and is interested in. Being involved in challenging, interesting, and trending assignments/projects that stimulate intellectual abilities, use mental faculties, and result in intellectual optimisation and enhancement is sought after by employees.

<table>
<tr><td>

4. Occupational wellness

</td></tr>
<tr><td>

"Occupational wellness is a healthy work-life balance that includes managing workplace obligations and stress as well as maintaining healthy relationships with co-workers. Workplace obligations are balanced by personal activities that allow for rest, relaxation, and connecting with friends and family" (Stride, n.d.).[37] Occupational wellness of employees is heavily dependent on a healthy, positive, and progressive organisational culture, authentic leadership, career development, and a fair and equitable compensation. Belonging to a value-based, people-centric employer branded organisation is the key contributor to employee wellness.

</td></tr>
<tr><td>

5. Social wellness

</td></tr>
<tr><td>

"Social wellness is achieved when we are able to create and maintain healthy, reciprocal relationships with the people around us. Positive social relationships can provide us with comfort and support in difficult times, increasing our resilience and ability to cope with life's challenges" (Stride, n.d.).[38] Social wellness largely stems from diversity and inclusivity, where a sense of belonging can be experienced in social groups. Societal awareness of all kinds of shaming is paramount. Bullying is frowned upon, shunned by societies, and taken seriously by communities, organisations, and authorities. Awareness is on the rise about cyberbullying, trolling, cancel culture, and the balance that one needs in social media interactions.

</td></tr>
<tr><td>

6. Financial Wellness

</td></tr>
<tr><td>

Adams (2023) states that "financial wellness is a relative measure of how well a person manages their financial life. Improving financial wellness is about practicing better money habits, setting goals, and taking steps to achieve them—all with the aim of improving your overall quality of life. This concept is about changing financial behaviors and adopting more effective money habits to secure financial stability and financial freedom."[39] Financial wellness of employees, reflected in the total rewards

</td></tr>
</table>

constituting financial and non-financial compensation, plays a key role. The sense of fairness as perceived and believed, based on the extent of fairness and equity in the employment exchange process, goes a long way in contributing to the financial well-being of employees. In addition, financial savings with sufficient flexibility in spending to have lifestyle choices and maintain contemporary social standards, is a motivator in seeking gainful employment for employees.

7. Environmental Wellness

According to Menke (2019), "environmental wellness refers to leading a lifestyle that values the relationship between ourselves, our community and the environment. The core principle of environmental wellness is respect—respect for all nature and all species living in it."[40] Environmental wellness is an area that has increased significantly, and organisations are implementing mandatory initiatives to contribute to the sustainable development goals. The focus is on environmental issues plaguing humankind and the importance of green/circular economy. The need for planet preservation and respecting the workings of Mother Earth, cannot be more emphasised for environmental wellness.

8. Spiritual Wellness

Brunton (2022) describes spiritual wellness "as a sense of interconnectedness and oneness with all life. It includes the development and use of personal values and beliefs to guide behavior, as well as a sense of purpose or meaning in life."[41] Spiritual wellness lies in realising the inner potential, being mindful of one's existence, living life to the fullest, and doing what one is meant to do. This is the current thinking of employees. Configured into this thinking is the role of humanity and the planet, which is being taken seriously by all generations. Getting involved in socially relevant projects, contributing to social causes, and functioning with a sense of justice is gaining prominence. A flexible blend of materialism and spiritualism is being adopted by people, for living life practically and by contributing to the bigger picture of one's existence realistically.

⇒ Professionalism and employee well-being

Recruiting professional managers, developing them, and enhancing their professionalism is the deciding factor and would give the right impetus to employee well-being and mental health. "Professionalism is a way of thinking, behaving, and appearing that demonstrates a commitment to excellence in all aspects of one's work. It encompasses a range of qualities, including a positive attitude, being coachable, taking responsibility for one's actions, displaying a strong work ethic, and exhibiting respect for others" (www.linkedin.com, 2022).[42] Professionalism, in its simplest form, is doing the job as per the requirements and standards of the job and, doing it ethically. Ethics are embedded in every profession. A professional is someone who has the highest work ethic towards work achievement and people management.

Professionals thrive in a professional environment and in the company of other professionals. Anything contrary to this may result in the professional leaving his/her professionalism or leaving the profession itself. This dynamic of unprofessionalism puts organisations in the vicious cycle of unprofessional behaviours and leads to widespread unprofessionalism among other organisations, as they benchmark with each other, peer observe one another, and determine the professional frame of reference. Professional managers contribute towards employee well-being by following the moral principles of life, through humane behavioural patterns, ethical responses, and fair people management practices. Unprofessional managers, on the contrary, may increase employee ill-being by grossly violating these aspects. The behaviours and characteristics of people managers that contribute to or violate employee well-being are listed in Table 3.

Table 3: Contributors to employee well-being and violators of employee well-being.

People managers' behaviours and characteristics

Contributors to employee well-being	Violators of employee well-being
Motivating	Demotivating
Energising	Draining
Developmental	Detrimental
Team interest	Self-interest
Credit giver	Credit taker
Proactive	Reactive
Mentally agile	Rigid
Transparent	Secretive
Growth mindset	Fixed mindset
Collaborative	Divisive
Fair	Unfair
Non-discriminatory	Discriminatory
Respectful	Disrespectful
Appreciative	Victimising
Knowledgable	Ignorant
Dedicated	Negligent
Humble	Arrogant

If not implemented effectively, well-being initiatives will be reduced to 'toothless and clawless tigers,' having no positive impact on the perpetrator or on the victim. In effect, it emboldens the perpetrators and validates their wrongdoings, as inaction or insufficient action on the part of management, tantamount to visibly condoning such actions rather than condemning them. It validates the behaviours and wrongdoings of perpetrators and leads to covertly encouraging this victimisation, as the victim who was wronged was not supported and the incident was not addressed fairly, or ignored, thereby perpetuating these wrongdoings. The hotlines and grievance procedures established by organisations are rendered **noiseless, voiceless, and useless**. This subsequently, results in the spread of toxic behaviours and wrongdoings and provides fodder for the growth of perpetrators.

The pressing need is to set up swift and fair redressal systems, supported by strong discouragement, overt disapproval, and vigilant leadership, which puts every effort into combating toxic/discriminatory behaviours. This will have more impact on employee engagement and employee retention than any other people management mechanism or best practice.

From the organisational point of view having, an effective and authentic leadership with progressive, positive, and inclusive behaviours and exhibiting the right values; people management practices with underlying principles of fairness, equity, and transparency; and a healthy work culture embracing diversity and inclusivity, contributes to employee well-being and collaborative work. These aspects should be embedded in the organisational architecture and systems and, inherently, be a part of the organisation culture.

> ✓ **A professional work environment made possible by professionals working for professional enhancement, will, in its purest form, contribute to employees' well-being.**
>
> ✓ **Employee well-being + Mental health = Healthy organisation.**

⇒ Quiet quitting and loud quitting

The broken psychological contract of employees, which is widespread in organisations, has found outlets through quiet quitting and loud quitting. "Quiet quitting is essentially a rejection of the idea that work has to take over your life and that you, as an employee, should be going above and beyond in your role. Instead, people are now reverting to only performing the duties outlined in their job description and politely declining to take on any more responsibilities outside of that or work longer hours than necessary" (Foster and News.com.au, 2022).[43]

Quiet quitting is reflected in employees' work performance, which would have changed from an 'exceeding expectations' to a 'meeting expectations' or 'below expectations' performance rating. Quiet quitters start to miss deadlines, put in minimum effort, are not interested in the outcomes, and stop having any expectations from the management, where in the real sense, their work commitment and spirit in the current job and organisation are dying or dead. They no longer express their concerns or highlight areas for improvement in the organisation. Quiet quitters crossed the threshold of hope, to a state of hopelessness.

According to Jackson (2023) "Loud quitters are "actively disengaged" at work, as opposed to quiet quitters, who are simply "not engaged."[44] Robinson (2023) states that "loud quitting is a workplace trend that involves an employee making a scene or openly expressing perceived negative aspects of their working experience before or during resignation."[45]

Loud quitters are vociferous and express, even more strongly than ever before, on the defective systems, unreasonable demands, impossible situations, unhelpful work patterns, toxic culture, unethical managerial practices, and unprofessional leadership styles. They try to be professionally assertive in their communication to drive home the point, but managers tend to term it as unprofessional aggression, either because of **arrogance**, **ignorance**, or **negligence** on their part. These managerial positions are self-destructive and erode the managerial credibility and leadership authenticity, while perpetuating toxicity and unprofessionalism.

It is in the interest of managers to convert these 'negatives' into positives. The quitters, both quiet and loud, should be identified and noticed for the right reasons, rather than, being identified and noticed for the wrong reasons, like for giving them a warning, blacklisting them, and labelling them as problem makers. They are looked upon as someone to be wary of and to be 'gotten rid of' as soon as possible. On the contrary, they should be identified and contacted to seek work improvement ideas about systems/processes, have discussions regarding healthy and positive culture creation, and consider their stand on managerial practices and ethical approach. These are right thinking employees, with professional expectations, and with good intentions of trying to set things right in the organisation. They are mistakenly, or deliberately ignored or sidelined with a punitive intention rather than that of a progressive, open minded, feedback seeking professional attitude.

Professional managers will use their power and authority to establish, set, and encourage professional work patterns, ethical practices, and a positive approach that contributes to the progress of the organisation. On the other hand, unprofessional managers misuse or abuse their power and authority, to alienate right-thinking employees who voice their concerns, and work in the best interests of the organisation. These employees' intention should be condoned, not condemned, failing to do so, would result in widespread quiet quitting and loud quitting. The best way to prevent or minimise quiet quitting and loud quitting is to right the wrong situations, or hire the right managers with the right values, mindset, and professionalism conducive to engaging and retaining quiet quitters and loud quitters. These quitters can be converted into engaged employees with positive actions from the leadership, one of them being quiet hiring. According to research it can be determined that:

> When employees "quiet quit," organizations keep people but lose skills and capabilities. Savvy organizations will turn this practice on its head and embrace "quiet hiring" as a way to acquire new skills and capabilities without adding new full-time employees. This will manifest as: Encouraging internal talent mobility by deploying employees to the areas where the organization most needs them. To compensate

people for their evolving roles, organizations can offer a one-time bonus, raise, additional paid time off, a promotion, greater flexibility, and more. Providing specific upskilling opportunities to help employees to meet evolving organizational needs. Leveraging alternate methods, such as alumni networks and gig workers, to bring in workers with specific skills for high-priority tasks when new headcount is not an option (McRae et al., 2023).[46]

In this age of social and professional media platforms and as the employees' right to well-being, 'quiet quitting and loud quitting' quit hosting organisations' premises, go viral, and travel globally. It becomes a monster created by organisations, which eventually devours them socially, professionally, and with all stakeholders concerned, subsequently leading to the decline or collapse of the organisation. A professional and progressive approach by managers will decrease quiet quitting and loud quitting, whereas an unprofessional and regressive approach by managers will perpetuate them (Figure 15).

1. Employees of different generations, place importance on value-based leadership that exhibits integrity and performs with authenticity. The prevailing leadership styles not aligned with this philosophy are regressive and will hinder employee engagement and employee retention in Business 5.0. Talent acquisition and talent management will be difficult for organisations in which leadership lacks integrity and authenticity.

Figure 15: Indicators of progressive approach and regressive approach of managers.

2. Fairness and equity, at all stages of the employee life cycle, and in all experiences and touchpoints, are the keys to success for organisations in Business 5.0. Current unfair work practices will function as hurdles in the way to success, unless and until they are converted to fair and equitable people management practices and implemented in the same spirit.

3. Inclusivity and non-discriminatory treatment on all fronts, for all employees, is the way forward, as the younger generations put more value to this aspect. Discriminatory practices and treatment indicate an outdated, negative, and inhuman approach on part of the management.

4. A healthy and positive work environment is the underlying factor contributing to employee engagement and employee retention. A toxic work environment in terms of leadership styles, communication patterns, and people management practices, will have a negative impact on employees' well-being.

5. Transparency and openness in all employee dealings, be it pay, promotion, training and development, or any other mechanism, are long overdue in many organisations. Secrecy in employee related matters and decisions that do not authenticate values, fairness, and equity do not bode well in Business 5.0. Employees are unable to perceive the authenticity and validity of these decisions unless there is transparency in the decision-making criteria, communication, and implementation.

6. Flexible work practices, a fast-growing trend, are a necessity in Business 5.0. Segmenting and customising work

practices according to the generation, function, competency cycle, portfolio mix, and talent type are more relevant. It is the work-life fit more than the work-life balance that people managers should consider. Rigid work practices or one blanket policy hinders talent development, talent progression, and talent management.

7. Career development and career growth opportunities determine talent engagement and talent retention. Providing career development and being innovative in formulating career pathways that support multi-disciplinary and multi-faceted employee profiles are relevant in Business 5.0. 'Moving up' or just 'keeping on moving' pathways in the same business function, different functional areas of work, or parallel pathways is what employees seek. This is essential to prevent them from 'moving out' of the organisation.

8. Performance based compensation operating on the principle of fairness, of being paid for the effort, outcome, and contribution, is the need of the day. Compensation practices being perceived as unfair, inadequate, and irrelevant to the competence and contribution of the employees are detrimental to employee engagement and employee retention in Business 5.0.

9. Psychological safety, where employees feel protected and treated with dignity and honour while being mindful of inclusivity, is the main motivator for them. Organisations in which psychological contracts are non-existent or broken will adversely impact employee engagement and employee retention in Business 5.0.

10. Employee well-being initiatives should form the underlying philosophy from which all other people management practices and culture creation emanate. Extra care, intense efforts, and vigilance should be put in each aspect of employee well-being. Identifying what contributes to and what has not worked well till now is crucial, as employee well-being is an ongoing process and an ever-changing aspect of Business 5.0.

⇒ **Global citizenship**

Business 5.0 is dominated by digital disruptions, changed business landscapes with short duration, and riddled with the expectations of the younger generations, who consider themselves global citizens. This calls for a massive transformation in management philosophy, strategic thinking, and culture creation, providing a work culture and environment in which this thought process is encouraged so global citizens can thrive. Oxfam (2021) states that "global citizenship is a term used to describe the social, environmental, and economic actions taken by individuals and communities who recognise that every person is a citizen of the world."[47]

According to McCarthy (2019), "Global Citizens believe in racial justice, gender equity, and climate justice. Global Citizens believe that we're all connected — a fact starkly illustrated by the COVID-19 pandemic, which threatens all of us until it threatens none of us — and that it's on us all to call for a just transition away from the status quo of rampant inequality and environmental degradation, toward a future of shared prosperity and environmental regeneration."[48]

People management practices, strategic direction, and leadership values supporting global citizenship are required. Business 5.0 environment and global conceptual frameworks make it possible for every right-thinking employee to be a global citizen. A widespread conceptual acceptance, systems implementation and leadership intent will grant employees the global citizenship status. According to research, it has been determined that:

> Global citizenship is also about shared values and shared responsibility. Global citizens understand that local events are significantly shaped and affected by global and remote events, and vice-versa. They champion fundamental human rights above any national law or identity, and social contracts that preserve elements of equality among all people. Diversity, interdependence, empathy, and perspective are essential values of global citizenship. Global citizens harness these values and are uniquely positioned to contribute to multiple contexts — locally, nationally, and internationally — without harming one community to benefit another. They foster and promote international understanding. Global citizens include individuals, corporations, global nomads, "glocals," young and old, big, and small, for-profit, and non-profit, public, and private, introverts and extroverts, men and women and children and anyone in between. Global citizenship and long-term, visionary leadership go together: Individual leaders who espouse shared values, and corporate citizens whose

governance, ethics, business model and investment strategy create — not only extract — value in each and every place they touch (Rinne, 2017).[49]

Awareness of the global citizenship concept should increase in the corporate world, as this signals changes in people management mechanisms. Changes in work attendance, flexibility in work timings, recognising employees' participation in global citizenship initiatives, and respecting and celebrating that work are empowering for global citizens, who constitute an integral part of the Business 5.0 workforce.

> ✓ **Every management deserves the employees they have, as they are responsible and accountable for creating a professional work environment conducive to employee well-being, employee engagement, and employee retention.**

06 | People Enablement

In Business 5.0, people managers are the facilitators and deciders, whereas technological advancements, virtual working, and data driven platforms, are the enablers and accelerators of work productivity. They enable people management practices to blend and lend to digital experiences and virtual interactions. Metaverse and cyber-technology-human interfaces are here to stay. The volume and value of data captured and stored are being increasingly assimilated by employees. People analytics and knowledge management lay the foundation for stakeholder value creation in Business 5.0.

⇒ Metaverse

Meta (2023) states that "the metaverse is the next evolution in social connection and the successor to the mobile internet. Like the internet, the metaverse will help you connect with people when you aren't physically in the same place and get us even closer to that feeling of being together in person.'[50] Allen (2022) explains that "the metaverse is an open ecosystem of tools that allow users to immerse themselves in digital environments and experience the world in new, impactful ways. Similar to the birth of the internet, it will influence how we work, play and shop, enhancing visual collaboration."[51]

It is imperative for people management professionals to get a grip on the enormous impact of the metaverse on employee roles and, self-assess if they have the capacity to bring in the transformation at the pace required for 'staying ahead' or 'keeping pace' with the collaborators in Business 5.0. This calls for a deep sense of urgency in transforming employee roles aligned to a metaverse induced Business 5.0, in which customer experiences and employee journeys are evolving to 'never-seen-before' happenings.

Vulpen (2022) explains that "as the metaverse redesigns the way we work, there could be major implications for HR leaders who should be driving this transformation. Not only do HR leaders have access to the necessary tools and know-how to implement this change but they also need to ensure the future of work is designed with people in mind."[52]

Onboarding, recruiting, learning and development, and other people management practices are heavily lending themselves to metaverse experiences. Digitalisation allows for the creation of virtual spaces and designing work patterns/arrangements that lead to a collaborative output, innovative thinking, and employee well-being that is aligned to Business 5.0.

Providing psychologically safe virtual work experiences and mitigating cybercrimes is the combined responsibility of employees, people managers, and cybersecurity professionals. In short, it is every employee's responsibility to report and share their online experiences, virtual concerns, and actively report any anomalies. This accelerates the digital transformation process at the pace and safety levels that the organisation requires.

⇒ **Cyber-technology-human blended workforce**

Presently, HR bots are assisting people management professionals with routine and administrative tasks. People management professionals are freed from mundane, repetitive, and first-level employee interactions to focus on analysing, interpreting, gauging, researching, and redesigning people management practices. They have the most scarce resource, which has been missing in their careers till now, **time**. The time to redirect their energies to progress better with the latest trends in the people management area. They can now channel their time, effort, and vigilance into how people management is changing, and forecast the developments that will occur, so they can be future-ready with appropriate people management mechanisms and practices.

The blended workforce created by collaborating with bots brings in its wake, the danger of inbuilt biases. The AI tools that support people managers in data input, data collation, data access, data interpretation, and data analytics need to operate on unbiased parameters and algorithms. Cyber audits and bot working configurations should be transparent and fall within the ethical practices espoused by the organisation. It should support the DEIB culture and operate on a fair, equitable, and unbiased platform.

⇒ **People analytics**

According to research (CIPD, 2022), it can be determined that "people analytics is about analysing data about people to solve business problems. It is sometimes called HR analytics or workforce analytics. It is defined as a number of processes, enabled by technology, which use descriptive, visual, and statistical methods to interpret people data and HR processes. You can find people data from HR systems, from other departments like IT, and from external sources such as salary surveys. You can use insights from people data to drive organisational change."[53]

People management professionals are positively inclined towards people analytics to overcome the challenges they are facing with people management issues and to make sense of the complexity of the data-driven Business 5.0 landscape. Their role in ensuring that the right type of employees, with the right mindset and skill sets are available at the right time, is evolving. They are using people related data to analyse talent acquisition, compensation, employee engagement, and employee retention parameters in people management. People analytics is providing scope for analysing employee well-being expectations, the impact of current practices, and the indication of processes, and work patterns, to be renewed or replaced.

"By analysing internal data, research, and studies, combined with expert judgment, experience, values, and concerns, HR can make evidence-based decisions rather than relying on a "feeling." This helps remove biases, temporary fixes, and inconsistencies" (AIHR, 2021).[54] People analytics are majorly categorised into four types, namely, descriptive analytics, diagnostic analytics, predictive analytics, and prescriptive analytics.

1. **Descriptive analytics** involves identifying and finding out 'what happened,' related to the occurrences and background information useful for decision making in

people management. This clarifies the patterns, connections, and historical data. Employee demographics, psychographics, employee turnover, employee absenteeism, workplace accidents, customer complaints, categories of performance evaluation, and similar data describing 'what is happening' and 'as it is happening' fall under this category.

2. **Diagnostic analytics** digs deeper into descriptive analytics; it examines the reasons why these patterns occur and finds out the causes of these happenings. It gives insights on management decision making, as it explores the interactions, connections, interconnections, anomalies, loopholes, and lapses by uncovering the root causes. It is more investigative in nature and aims to discover the causes of employee data and patterns. These analytics decipher reasons for employee disengagement, employee turnover, absenteeism, presenteeism, different performance categories, and related areas.

3. **Predictive analytics** are based on descriptive and diagnostic analytics and inform people managers as to what can recur or is likely to occur in the future. A good indicator for taking 'moving away' or 'moving ahead' decisions to mend the situation or reap benefits from it. The past has an impact on the present, and the present has a bearing on the future. This analysis helps in predicting the patterns that may form in people management, forecasting future occurrences and trend extrapolations, which may improve the decision-making process of people managers.

4. **Prescriptive analytics** is the next step based on predictive analytics. It is the stage in which decisions are made, initiatives are finalised, and plans related to people management are formulated. It supports decision-making to achieve the best results and expected outcomes in people management.

According to research (CIPD, 2018) "people analytics is rising up the agenda for organisations globally. With technology providing businesses more and more ways to collect people data, using this information to gain workforce insight, drive business performance and enhance employee experience is expected to grow."[55]

⇒ **Knowledge management**

The concept of knowledge management is an area of interest that has not yet reached its full potential, as the nature of knowledge is ever changing and evolving. Dixon (2017) categorised the three eras of knowledge management as leveraging explicit knowledge, leveraging experiential knowledge, and leveraging collective knowledge,[56] which form the basis for knowledge management initiatives in Business 5.0. It is a combination of all three components (eras), with each component taking a share of total knowledge management, based on the progress and stage of development of knowledge management in that organisation.

1. **Explicit knowledge** is the accuracy and understanding of knowledge. It is knowledge that is clearly communicated, shared, stored, and used, contributing to information management, thereby enhancing individual learning, and improving employee capabilities.

2. **Experiential knowledge** is the first-hand experience, incidental information, effort and outcome experiences, human feelings and behavioural patterns connected to work. It is related to experience management and knowledge transfer through teams, groups, and communities for group productivity and work improvements.

3. **Collective knowledge** is the team and organisational level knowledge, reflected in data, information, decisions, systems, processes, and experiences, as a cumulative impact and summation of all areas of knowledge and experiences. It is related to idea management, drawing on collective knowledge, experiences, and thought processes aimed at building organisational capability.

In the Business 5.0 landscape, with the interface of technological advancements and human experiences, these three knowledge components will continue to evolve. Collating, building, and capitalising on knowledge is the lifeline to success in the Business 5.0 environment. Sourcing and optimising the use of digital data and analytical capabilities is gaining momentum. Collective intelligence and knowledge management, leading to intellectual capital and business superiority, are critical resources that are not available in the right volume and value, as expected in organisations. The attention it deserves cannot be more emphasised as it is a vital contributor in making or breaking organisations in this information age. According to research:

> More and more organisations are depending on capitalising on existing resources as the workplace needs are changing rapidly. Intellectual capital and knowledge networks play a critical role in effectively man-

aging those rapid changes and help organisations sustain through the changes and competition. Learning and development function is seen as a key driving force to build knowledge capital in the organisation. The purpose has shifted from being a training provider to a strategic function and an enabler for the organisation to maintain a long-term sustainable competitive advantage (Kumar Anne, 2021).[57]

In effect, underdeveloped and incomplete knowledge management systems not only have an adverse impact on organisations, but have repercussions on talent acquisition in the industry, as well. "The resulting reduction in knowledge transfer and continued talent shortfalls for local companies has reduced growth and dynamism over time, reducing the capacity of local labour markets" (World Economic Forum, 2018).[58] Moving forward, the Business 5.0 environment would continue to be characterised by industry convergence, multi-specialism, stakeholder value creation, and employee agile thinking. This necessarily implies that every organisation should have robust knowledge capture, knowledge collation, knowledge renewal, knowledge transfer, knowledge usage, and knowledge retrieval systems in place. Business 5.0 is connected to leveraging knowledge management systems, contributing to the Business 5.0 ecosystem.

> ✓ **Knowledge flow of all types, to all generations, from all generations is essential for success in Business 5.0.**

07 | People Management Practices

Human resources management in Business 5.0 is holistically viewed as people management, where employees are not just considered as resources to the organisation but are treated as people, whose differences, similarities, aspirations, and frustrations play a significant role in shaping people management practices. Differentiated policies catering to hybrid work patterns and arrangements, inclusive recruitment and selection processes, fair and equitable compensation, and meaningful career development, in addition to having fulfilling employee journeys and mindful employee touch points, would strengthen the people management practice.

⇒ Workforce trends

The future employee workforce will, majorly, comprise freelancers, short-term, and part-time contract workers. Rehiring separated employees, which was earlier frowned upon by many organisations, is in vogue now. Welcoming 'boomerang' employees to tap the experiences they acquired in other organisations, is a significant shift, in the hiring process of people management. Recruitment processes are breaking all forms of rigidity and are aimed at sourcing the right talent, at the right time, to be placed in the right jobs. The talent search is magnanimous in nature, as it hires new talent or rehires old talent with new refinement. Some interesting trends in resourcing are, tapping the passion economy and the hidden workforce:

> Venture capital firm Andreessen Horowitz published a report on the future of work. One of its key findings is that the gig economy and the "Uber for X" model are partly making way for the passion economy, where micro-entrepreneurs monetize their individuality and creativity. A key reason for the growth of the passion economy is that it offers alternative ways of making money, innovative paths toward professional fulfilment and unprecedented career opportunities for millennials (World Economic Forum, 2022).[59]

People managers need to invest in a workforce that has often been ignored, the hidden workforce:

> The hidden workforce, also known as the "forgotten workforce," represents workers and includes retirees who want to work, caregivers, neurodiverse individuals, people with long-term health problems (including those with long Covid), ex-inmates, and people without degrees. These either already participate in the workforce but want to work more (and are often paid as "hourly workers") or do not participate yet but are willing to work under the right conditions (van Vulpen, 2020).[60]

Traditionally, it was lifetime employment that both employers and employees aimed for. Earlier, an employee taking up two or three jobs in a 40-year career was labelled a job hopper.

The trend now is that if an employee is in one job for more than 3-5 years, the employee's career is stagnant, assuming that the employee is doing the same work in the same manner and may have become redundant. This does not necessarily mean that employees should move jobs every 3-5 years, but implies bringing in changes and changed work systems, enriching, and enlarging the current job, making their jobs dynamic, and proving that they are not redundant. With technological advancements, all jobs and work systems have changed, giving employees the versatility in their jobs to prevent career obsolescence in Business 5.0.

⇒ **Hybrid policies**

People management has moved from the traditional one blanket (catch-all) policy, at least in one area, which is in the employee work attendance patterns. Post pandemic, most organisations have implemented hybrid work attendance policies for employees. Blanket policies are not suited for the requirements of a multigenerational workforce. With the multigenerational workforce expectations and their differences in work patterns, it is essential for organisations to formulate differentiated generation-wise, group-wise, talent segment-wise policies linked to the work profiles. This will align better with each talent segment/age group, resulting in employee engagement and employee retention.

The future trends are having multiple policies catering to multiple groups and generations in the organisations, and differentiated policies customised to different talent segments of the workforce. Multiple policies are not a new concept in the corporate sector, for instance, health insurance benefits extended to family members of a married employee, overtime/ risk allowance paid to employees who work under different/ difficult conditions, and such related policies, are already existing. Differentiated policies ensuring fairness and equity, as opposed to, equality and uniformity, tend to be more meaningful in managing a multigenerational and different talent segments of the workforce. People management practices must cater to the specific requirements of each broad generational group, based on their similarities, and broken down into specific talent segments and subgroups, related to their differences. This gives the dual benefit of, specifically, attracting and retaining different talent segments. Employees of different generations and talent segments would seek the employer of their choice based on the IEVP.

⇒ Employee resourcing

Digital transformation signifies strategic changes and revamped business models. Redesigning systems and business remodelling aligned to the fast-changing Business 5.0 landscape, incorporating the dynamism of the markets, and shifting customer preferences, is gaining relevance. It is vital to provide as 'good,' or 'best,' or 'better than' the product offerings than those of collaborators in the market. This requires having employees with the skill sets, mindset, and rare talents who can cope with the evolving dynamics and achieve the strategic goals. The talent requirements are shifting rapidly, and the ability to source such talent is on the upside. Relevant employer rebranding and becoming the employer of choice, are crucial aspects to consider in talent acquisition, for success in Business 5.0.

Traditional recruitment processes based on fixed recruitment drives and calendar plans, like semi-annual or annual recruitment drives, will not suffice. The need is to plan continuously with a focus on parameters such as, the type of talent segments, talent availability, and location preferences of these talent segments. It is, on-time recruiting, happening in real-time.

A multi-source agile recruitment process is recommended. According to Drake (2020), "demand for talent is converging on critical roles, so when the required talent is identified, it is taking too long to secure it and driving higher cost. Taking an Agile approach to talent acquisition can better enable and meet the needs of the business. Agile creates and fosters high performing, customer-centric HR teams utilising the Agile culture and tools to meet the demand for rapid, collaborative, and transparent recruitment processes."[61] It can be stated that:

> Talent acquisition today requires an agile recruiting approach that can anticipate and meet the changing needs of the business. This new operating model delivers a range of improvements in hiring measures by using continuous planning, a predictive hiring process and talent-focused design. For example, a predictive hiring process can reduce time to fill, especially for new-to-firm roles. It has been taking longer and longer to fill roles in recent years. That is a result of the heightened demand for talent in general, but it also reflects the specific challenge for recruiters of hiring for more specialized roles, roles with which they are unfamiliar and a mix of roles that keeps

changing. A more agile approach is especially critical if talent acquisition is going to support business strategy. Without it, recruiting teams will be unable to understand the new positions for which they are hiring, anticipate changes in supply or mitigate talent supply risks (Wiles, 2019).[62]

It is talent-centric resourcing rather than filling in business-projected vacancies, which will significantly support sourcing employees for hard-to-fill jobs. With the emerging jobs, the focus is on matching talent segment requirements with talent availability, which is made possible through agile recruiting. An agile recruiting process that facilitates matching the intricate talent segments, filling mission-critical positions, and resourcing talent aligned to Business 5.0 challenges and specifications is the best way forward.

Focusing on 'talent portfolios' rather than just 'jobs' is gaining recognition. The source to tap for these potential employees is also different. A multi-source availability is being explored, thereby changing the entire recruiting process. The quest of people managers is for the right talent sources from which to access these talent pools. The more suitable sources of recruitment are social and professional media platforms, e-channels, and organisations' website. Employee referrals also play a huge role in hiring talented people.

⇒ **Employee selection**

The time-tested selection methods for meeting people management plans have given way to customised, individualised selection techniques specific to each talent segment or individual talent profile. Background checks, professional record and potential assessments form the basis for employee selection. The top ten selection criteria on which candidates are likely to be assessed in Business 5.0 employment selection are listed in Table 4 .

Table 4: Selection criteria

Futuristic approach
Business acumen
Technology savvy
Digital leadership
Stakeholder centricity
Multicultural collaboration
Mental agility
Resilience
Design thinking
Intrapreneurship

Selecting candidates, especially at the entry level, would most probably, involve gamification and use of trending interactive virtual platforms that are familiar to younger generations. For experienced generations, it takes the form of performance profiling, achievement records, potential reviews, and personality assessments. For all generations, the starting point may include cyber-technology experiences, as this would set the tone for candidates on how the work patterns are unfolding.

⇒ **Career development**

Career development starts with employee onboarding and placement. There is a perceptible shift in employees' career paths and career growth. Traditional career development involved promotions, salary increases, and titled positions. Moving forward, career advancement would mean professional enhancement, expanding competency bases, acquiring the right talent mix, and multi-specialism. Employees are inclined towards employers who provide flexibility in vertical, horizontal, cross-functional, and new function career pathways. Career development takes the shape of new assignments, interesting work, challenging projects, and just fulfilling the need to be in emerging fields that are of interest to employees.

Employees would be better integrated with organisations that provide the mobility to move within the organisation, undertake projects/assignments where their talent mix could be matched. This mobility is not restricted to organisations but extends to the local, regional, and global markets. Talented employees are marketable, and their talent profiles are not only bankable within the organisation but also within the industry and among relevant industries, as applicable. Christian (2023) opines "during the height of talent shortages, disgruntled workers could more easily vote with their feet, job hopping or industry switching to find roles they enjoyed."[63]

Figure 16: Employee mobility and marketability

The younger generations are more likely to consider themselves global employees. This is not just because of remote working/digital systems but also because of their mindset. In spirit, they connect globally and with ease, due to the travel experiences and virtual interactions they are exposed to.

✓ **Previously, it was local employees working in global organisations.**

✓ **Currently, it is global employees working in local organisations.**

⇒ **Compensation**

Historically, compensation was the key factor that employees considered in employment. It has been the main deal-breaker or dealmaker in employee engagement and employee retention and will continue to be so in the future. Though the types and categories of compensable factors are changing, compensation per se, as a reward component, would remain a prominent people management focus area, and top priority for talent attraction, talent engagement, and talent retention. Research determines that:

> One of the major shifts in compensation management is the move from paying for jobs and titles to paying for skills and competencies. This means rewarding employees based on the value they create and the capabilities they demonstrate, rather than on their seniority or position. This approach can help you adapt to changing market demands, support employee development and career mobility, and foster a culture of learning and innovation. To implement this strategy, you need to define the skills and competencies that are critical for your organization, assess your employees' current and potential levels, and design pay structures and incentives that reflect their contributions (www.linkedin.com, 2023).[64]

The shift is from a position-based pay to a competency-based compensation. This would fit well and be in line with the expectations of employees belonging to different segments and having varying talent portfolio mixes, as compensation packages would be customised based on their contribution and suiting their requirements. Therefore, incorporating variability within compensation packages would support talent attraction and talent retention. Organisations can overcome long prevailing malpractices in compensation by basing compensation decisions on performance data and people metrics, giving meaningful and complete rationale for compensation decisions. According to research:

> Strategic reward is based on the design and implementation of reward policies and practices that support and advance both the organisation's business and people objectives, and employee aspirations. Total reward covers all aspects of work that are valued by people, including such aspects as flexible working opportunities, or being rewarded fairly, in addition to the pay and benefits package. Total reward has implications for cultural change as it can focus in part on employee empowerment. (CIPD, 2023c).[65]

Financial and non-financial compensation are still the main components of a reward strategy. A total reward strategy in terms of segment-wise compensation with multiple options and choices for employees to select what suits their lifestyle and family requirements most, is recommended. It should encompass biodiversity and neurodiversity compensable factors. It may take the form of a sophisticated cafeteria-style menu. Gaille (2020) states, "cafeteria plans, also called Section 125 plans (US based), are growing in popularity. Their introduction came during the early 1980s when flexible benefits became a priority for workers."[66] The increasing need is to revamp fixed and rigid compensation structures with flexible plans. Different employee categories have different requirements based on their demographics, psychographics, and other backgrounds. They need options and different benefits suiting their current background, with the flexibility to switch to other available benefits as their status changes and so would their requirements.

According to Jansen (2022) "Pay Transparency Will Continue To Be At The Forefront Of Compensation Discussions."[67] As opposed to the current trend of compensation packages and reward decisions being confidential, the trend is to have inherently equity-based compensation packages that are transparent to employees thereby demonstrating commitment towards fairness and equity. It is vital for employees to perceive that they are associated with an employer who consolidates fairness and equity not just in the content of compensation, but also in its contextual application. The starting point is for employees to have knowledge of the compensation packages and plans. This will increase employee engagement and validate that the employer believes in equity, transparency, and fairness.

In addition, one major shift is in corporate social responsibility (CSR), an area which was grossly neglected and adversely impacted CSR initiatives, as employees' contribution towards this end was not fully captured, nor was it fully rewarded. Employee contributions to, and participation in CSR initiatives need to be captured, recognised, and rewarded. This is one way in which a collaborative employee approach locally, regionally, and globally will have a wider impact on the organisation's ESG initiatives.

> ✓ **A pressing need for organisations to 'walk the talk' about transparency starts with sharing information related to compensation with employees.**

⇒ Employee journeys

The employee journey starts when the employee sends in the job application for employment, joins the organisation and ends when the employee is totally separated from the organisation, both contractually and financially. The time duration, substantiated by the experiences that the employee has, and situations which he/she faces, can be considered as the employee journey. Vulpen (2018) outlines "the employee journey is the time an employee spends at a company, starting when the employee applies to the organization and ending when the employee quits the organization. All the time in between these two moments and the experiences that the employee has is the employee journey."[68]

The success of the employee journey is validated through people management practices, their positivity, and their progressiveness. More importantly, the focus is on career development prospects and compensation packages. The talent management philosophy, fairness, equity, and transparency are reflected in how career development is facilitated on an individual level, and in how the individual is being compensated, the adequacy of it and the flexibility it offers.

Nelson (2022) states that "when your employee experience reflects your organization's one-of-a-kind values and mission, every interaction employees have with you is authentic, inspires commitment and supports performance."[69] Employee journeys, like all other stakeholder journeys, are interactions, major and minor, significant, and insignificant. These interactions are characterised by two major components, the **transaction**, and the **treatment**. The transaction component is the business/economic aspect, whereas the treatment component is the psychological/behavioural aspect. Even if the transaction is successful and the treatment is not, employees and other stakeholders may not be inspired or engaged. If the treatment is effective, and the transaction is not, there may still be some degree of engagement in it. If both the transaction and the treatment are good, the employee interactions lead to better employee engagement.

✓ **Employee journeys are getting shorter.**
✓ **Employee interactions will lead to better employee engagement if both the transaction and treatment are effective, and meet or exceed employee expectations, both economically and psychologically.**

⇒ Employee touchpoints

"A touchpoint is a point of contact and/or engagement between a business and a customer. This type of contact/engagement can occur at any time throughout a customer's journey" (Indicative, n.d.).[70] This has been extended to all stakeholders, the most important of them being the employees, who are the internal customers. According to Vita (2022) "a good engagement strategy must start with identifying all touch points between the company and its staff to ensure that every effort is being made to meet employee needs. Otherwise, there is always the risk that problems and inefficiencies unknown to the HR department will undermine employee motivation and productivity."[71] The employee touchpoints to be mindful of, start even before the employee is hired, and extend till the employee is separated from the organisation. An illustrative list of employee touchpoints is given in Table 5.

Table 5 : Employee touchpoints

Fundamental areas	Touchpoints
Resourcing talent	• Aimed at attracting the right fit employees with the required talent mix.
Pre-recruitment	• Neutrally worded job vacancy announcements aligned to diversity and inclusivity policies. • Providing sufficient job role and compensation information. • Quick and personalised response to the job application status. • Having clear and valid recruitment criteria.
Selection	• Using reliable and valid methods for customised talent segment selection. • Quick and agile selection procedures. • Fair, transparent, and evidence-based communication related to employee selection. • Two-way communication for assessing employment suitability on both sides.

Fundamental areas	Touchpoints
Onboarding	• Complete information exchange relevant for new joiners. • Trending onboarding experiences.
Placement	• Projects/assignments/portfolio allocation based on expertise/talent mix. • Mutually accepted placement duration.
Learning and development	• Right skilling opportunities. • Ongoing developmental programmes. • Work environment is conducive to apply learning. • Lifelong learning culture.
Career development	• Clarity in career development opportunities and career growth. • Career pathways laid in all directions and aligned to multi-specialism. • Criteria for career pathways are fair, valid, and reliable.
Performance evaluation	• Performance dimensions and standards are communicated effectively. • Performance evaluations are fair and transparent. • Two-way communication during performance appraisals. • Performance evaluations are conducted in a professional manner.

Fundamental areas	Touchpoints
Compensation	• Fair and equity-based compensation criteria. • Consistency and transparency in compensation decisions. • Compensation is linked to employee contribution, productivity, and performance outcomes.
Organisational culture	• Progressive and professional organisational culture. • Positive and healthy work environment. • Non-threatening and psychologically safe environment.
Leadership style	• Authentic and value based. • People-centric. • Role model.
Communication patterns	• Two-way professional communication. • Inclusive and participative in nature. • Elicit feedback from all sources.
Collaborative work	• Teamworking and teambuilding. • Synergistic relationships.
Technological advancements and adoption	• Adopting technological systems and cyber-secure workspaces. • Support and time given to familiarise and adapt to technological advancements.
Separation	• Smooth and positive employee exit procedures.

Employee journeys and employee touchpoints contribute to employee engagement and employee retention. According to research:

> The several reasons why employee retention should be a top priority for any organization. First and foremost, it saves time and money. When an employee leaves, it can cost up to 200% of their salary to replace them. This includes the cost of advertising the job, interviewing candidates, and training new hires. Therefore, investing in a robust employee retention plan can save your organization significant amounts of money in the long run. Secondly, high employee turnover rates can have a significant impact on team morale. When employees see their colleagues leaving frequently, it can lead to feelings of instability and uncertainty. They may begin to wonder if their own job is secure, or if they should start looking for other opportunities. This can create a sense of disengagement and demotivation, leading to a drop in productivity and an increase in absenteeism (Baird, 2023).[72]

✓ **Ensuring that employee touchpoints meet the varied requirements of the multigenerational workforce and appeal to the different talent segments, is fundamental to efficacious people management and effective employee retention.**

PART

3

TALENT TRENDS

Chapters

8   Talent Development 113

9   Talent Management 127

10   Business 5.0 Competency Framework....................135

08 | Talent Development

Skill life cycles are getting shorter, thereby magnifying the need for reskilling and upskilling employees on a continuous basis. Having a new skilling strategy paves the way for ongoing initiatives and continuous implementation of these initiatives to capture changes occurring in Business 5.0. The learning and development function is characterised by lifelong learning, providing the right impetus for employees to acquire relevant mindsets and skill sets. Learning and development professionals need to foster a lifelong learning culture. The focus is on a mindset and skill sets that are transferable and facilitate vertical, horizontal, cross functional, and new function career growth. The lifelong learning culture, by default, brings in mental agility and the required mindset among employees, apart from bridging the skills gap for sustainable development in Business 5.0. According to Patnaik (2022) "skills decay at an exponential rate in the L&D space. Hence it is crucial to keep an eye on top trending skills that L&D requires to speed up skill development for the employees at diverse levels. The key skills are change readiness skills, instructional design skills, and researching skills."[73]

⇒ **Key skills**

The World Economic Forum–Future of Jobs 2023 report identified twenty-six key skills that would, as estimated, be in demand and primarily bridge the skills gap until the year 2027. This skills gap provides a compelling case for reskilling and upskilling employees in Business 5.0, as this skills gap is, in general, comparable to the skills gap which all sectors face. Reskilling and upskilling in these areas should be done on a priority basis.

Table 6 : Key Skills: 2023-2027

1.	Analytical thinking
2.	Creative thinking
3.	AI and big data
4.	Leadership and social influence
5.	Resilience, flexibility, and agility
6.	Curiosity and lifelong learning
7.	Technological literacy
8.	Design and user experience
9.	Motivation and self-awareness
10.	Empathy and active listening
11.	Talent management
12.	Service orientation and customer service
13.	Environmental stewardship
14.	Resource management and operations
15.	Marketing and media
16.	Networks and cybersecurity
17.	Dependability and attention to detail
18.	Systems thinking
19.	Programming
20.	Teaching and mentoring
21.	Multi-lingualism
22.	Manual dexterity, endurance, and precision
23.	Global citizenship
24.	Reading, writing and mathematics
25.	Quality control
26.	Sensory-processing abilities

Source: WEF_Future_of_Jobs_2023.pdf

⇒ Cybersecurity skills

Digital disruptions and technological advancements are moving at an extremely fast pace. Cyberattacks and the need for cybersecurity are also moving at an equally fast and parallel pace. Keeping data safe in the complex labyrinth of data storage systems and capabilities is a crucial aspect of an organisation's survival in the Business 5.0 environment. Any breach or leakage of data has long-reaching repercussions and is catastrophic in the current business scenario, where stakeholders' private and life-changing information can be mis-spread, misused, and misrepresented causing havoc in their lives. This has a domino effect on employees' employment status, customers' confidence, and organisation's survival. Cybersecurity is not just the function of cybersecurity professionals, it is the responsibility of all employees. Training employees in this area, will mitigate risks and allow organisations to operate with the confidence and knowledge that their operations and data are safe from global cyberattacks and threats. The inbuilt agility and security systems will support employees in functioning and focusing on business operations, knowing that they are in a cybersecure space and protected from cybercrimes plaguing the cyberworld. It is evident that:

> Business and cyber leaders are most closely aligned in their perspectives on emerging technology. Most organizational leaders appreciate that several fields of emerging technology, such as the use of machine learning, are being implemented at speed, used across a widening range of processes, and will affect their organization's cyber-risk profile. The implementation of new technologies will be undertaken in combina-

tion, significantly increasing the complexity of an organization's digital environment, and highlighting the need to embed cyber-risk management through all stages of a digital transformation process. Organizations must balance the value of new technology and the potential cyber exposure that comes with it to effectively manage their risk in the coming years. Smaller firms were more likely to suffer from a lack of the trained cybersecurity experts needed to manage internal risk. Cross-sectorial resilience measures, such as cyberthreat information sharing, were of less value due to the same cyber skills and capacity issues. Cyber and business leaders still have a great deal of work to do to truly understand each other, articulate the risk cyber issues pose to their business and translate that into meaningful management and mitigation measures. As the cyber landscape promises to become more complex in the coming years, it is critical that organizations work to resolve this now if they are to build systemic cyber resilience for the long term (Global Cybersecurity Outlook 2023, 2023).[74]

⇒ **New skilling**

In effect, talent acquisition costs more than talent development. The direct and indirect costs linked to external recruitment make internal recruitment more appealing. Talent development through a new skilling strategy would lead to improved motivation at an employee level. On the business front, it gets translated into major business outcomes like employee engagement, employee retention, sustainable development, business continuity, and organisational agility. It paves the way for current success and future survival.

Navarra (2022) states that "talent acquisition is more expensive than talent development. According to new benchmarking data from the Society for Human Resource Management (SHRM), the average cost per hire can be three to four times the position's salary. Soft costs which include the time and effort allocated by hiring managers in supporting the hiring process is about 60%."[75] The need is for new skilling. Employees need to be reskilled and upskilled to keep abreast of the changes occurring in Business 5.0 as:

The demand for skilled talent is only going to continue to grow, and the skills gap will only widen as technology advancements and societal shifts disrupt the status quo. The new world of work requires people to continuously hone their skills to stay relevant and improve their employability. The term new skilling represents all types of continuous learning to help build high-demand skills, whether an individual is trying to upskill current capabilities, or they need complete reskilling to build entirely new capabilities. A new skilling mindset keeps both a workforce and a company agile by ensuring learning initiatives are relevant to future business objectives and tailored to the needs of learners. This is simply the new reality—no business will survive for long without reskilling and upskilling initiatives driven by a new skilling strategy. By regularly identifying what skills will be needed in the future and which of those employees currently possess, organisations can build more thoughtful, continuous skilling programs to effectively develop those abilities in their workforce (www. cornerstoneondemand.com, n.d.).[76]

Reskilling for anticipated job changes and new jobs and upskilling for current and near future performance output are contributors that keep the talent pipelines **active**, **relevant**, and **alive**. The demand for emerging jobs and hard-to-fill jobs can be addressed through reskilling and upskilling of employees. The best way to cope with ongoing digital disruptions and thrive in the Business 5.0 environment requires a new skilling strategy encompassing reskilling, upskilling, and the right skilling of employees. Industry-technology convergence and industry convergence have catapulted new skills into the limelight. Business 5.0 mindsets and skill sets strengthen talent pipelines and impact talent development.

The cost-effective method to bridge the skills gap impacting the corporate world is through reskilling and upskilling. Reskilling and upskilling are beneficial not only to organisations in terms of increased profitability, enhanced productivity, and a better corporate image, but also to employees in terms of career progression and sustained employability. It mitigates the risk of losing employees who were effective to date, but are rendered redundant, because they were not upskilled or reskilled. This has a cumulative positive effect on employee engagement and employee wellbeing, especially for the younger generations.

"Lack of learning opportunities will make Gen Zers a flight risk. Learning opportunities are a top factor in Gen

Z's job hunt—showing that Gen Zers prioritize career development and find learning benefits highly appealing. So, it makes sense that learning opportunities can play an important role in retaining young workers. Gen Zers who did not receive workplace training are more likely to quit than those who received training" (TalentLMS, n.d.).[77]

⇒ **Learning and development trends**

Traditional long duration training is now giving way to microlearning and nano-learning. Currently, personalised learning, digital platforms' offerings, and bite-size scrolling are popular. Learning and development professionals need to proactively follow the trends in the training and learning fields. Micro-credentialing is giving employees the flexibility of time and attention, suitable to them, to fit bite-size learning into their learning agenda and further their career through new skilling. The main methods of learning relevant to Business 5.0 are referenced below.

- **Work-based learning [WBL]:** "Work-based learning courses and opportunities are designed and developed in partnership with employers, learners, and other stakeholders (where appropriate) and contain learning outcomes that are relevant to work objectives. Work-based learning consists of structured opportunities for learning and is achieved through authentic activity and is supervised in the workplace" (www.qaa.ac.uk, n.d.).[78]

- **Microlearning:** "Microlearning is the breaking down of information into small, bite-sized chunks so learners can easily absorb the information. Microlearning is typically delivered in small increments, meaning the learner tackles concepts in as little as five or ten minutes. The results mean that engagement rates soar from an average of 15% up to 90%. Learners can have a deeper understanding of the content at hand as well as apply the knowledge in practical and effective ways. Because of microlearning's effectiveness, eight out of 10 L&D professionals' favour microlearning above other learning methods because their learners prefer it" (Digipro Education Limited, n.d.).[79]

- **Nano-learning:** "Nano-learning is like the small sibling of Microlearning. Nano-learning is a highly targeted learning method designed to help people understand subject topics through smaller inputs in short time frames. Like the Microlearning concept of 'bite-size' learning or 'chunking,' it breaks down complex topics into digestible chunks. The idea is to deliver short and simple concepts in an engaging format. This is an effective method for content consumption through social media" (Digipro Education Limited, n.d.).[80] "A growing learning modality, nano learning is a way to deliver condensed information in an engaging format" (Laverty, 2020).[81]

- **Micro-credentials:** 'Micro-credentials are bite-sized qualifications that demonstrate skills, knowledge and/or experience in a specific subject area or capability' (Perna, 2021).[82] Micro-credentials are defined as: "short, stackable courses that learners—whether students, employees, or organization members—take to develop specific skills in their field. Because micro-credentials target skills in high-growth fields (such as IT support, project management, UX design, and cybersecurity), they can also have a major impact on an employee's competitive advantage within your company" (Karb, 2022).[83]

These latest learning trends are characterising the learning and development events and are becoming a priority rather than an option. They are forming an integral part of the learning and development function and employee learning journeys.

⇒ **Learning journey**

There is a perceptible shift in employee development, where it is a combination of trending learning events snowballing into a lifelong learning process, leading to sustained employability in Business 5.0 and the next norm. Lifelong learning, mapped with learning events and experiences, through a mix of work-based learning, microlearning, and nano-learning, leading to worthwhile and relevant credentials should be the top priority in Business 5.0. Nobels and Baele (2022b) state that "learning and development needs to think about how learning can be integrated in the flow of work, so that the workforce and business is able to grow as much as possible given shorter, faster, and integrated learning. Learning in the flow of work, working in the flow of learning."[84] Individual personal and professional development plans pave the way for a progressive and continuing learning journey. The learning journey is a fast-moving conveyor belt lined with evolving learning areas, learning options, learning events, and learning experiences.

⇒ **Bilateral/mutual coaching**

Coaching is a key development in the corporate world, which has now become mainstream and not sidelined anymore. Its popularity extends from job seekers to C-suite professionals and beyond. According to Hayden (2022) "coaching aims to produce optimal performance and improvement at work. It focuses on specific skills and goals and may also have an impact on an individual's personal attributes such as social interaction or confidence. The process typically lasts for a defined period or forms the basis of an on-going management style."[85]

Reverse coaching arrangements, in which the younger generations (Millennials and Generation Z) are coaching the earlier generations (Baby Boomers and Generation X), have given way to a bilateral coaching process, taking the shape of mutual coaching as every generation needs to learn from every other generation, be it earlier or younger. All employees have their strengths, lessons they learnt, and challenges they overcame, irrespective of the generation to which they belong. The nature, content, and context may differ, but challenges do remain and recur. Corporate life is marked by a collaborative approach among employee groups. The workplace trends are now synergistic, drawing on the talents and areas of expertise of earlier generations and those that of the younger generations.

In essence, it is the coaching of digital immigrants by digital natives, and vice versa, that facilitates talent optimisation. The industry knowledge, technological expertise, processes, systems, business acumen, problem solving, and cumulative knowledge of the digital immigrants can be tapped and transferred to the younger generations. In turn, the digital natives who are more tech savvy, creative, and inclusive, and know the changing customer experiences, as recipients and participants themselves, can give their input and share their knowledge. According to studies:

> Gen-Z may be unlike any other generation before, their skill set is also incredibly unique. Growing up in the age of technology, they are the first generation to have unlimited access to the internet, social media and technology. Gen-Z may be poised to be the most influential generation to foster transformation through technology, and I think businesses should use their special skills to their advantage through digital platforms, outreach and understanding the intricacies of our increasingly online world (D'Incerti, 2022).[86]

The input from both the earlier and younger generations will give the insights needed to successfully wade through the digital transformation and navigate the transformed markets.

⇒ Role of learning and development professionals

People managers and learning and development professionals' roles have changed significantly. The function and the role direction remain the same, but the context in which they are performed has dramatically changed. In the digitally disruptive environment, the role of learning and development professionals is to develop employees for emerging and non-existent jobs. Learning and development professionals are now spearheading learning and development initiatives for sustenance in a globally competitive and digitally disruptive environment.

The talent development strategy is an integral part of the Business 5.0 strategy. These professionals must create a learning culture and foster an environment in which employee learning can be applied. Laying the foundation for a learning culture and building on it requires a futuristic approach and reimagining learning in the future.[87] A concentrated, and structured learning, integrating a flexible development approach, is the need of the day. For this to materialise, it is imperative that learning and development professionals adopt similar learning journeys for themselves, giving them the professional insight to facilitate employees' development. It is important that:

> Reflection on how learning and development in organisations needs to adapt to this is required. The people profession needs to role-model continual learning in their own development. Key areas identified as capability gaps among the profession and people teams are agility, change management, courage to challenge, data and analytics skills and curiosity in exploration of data, ethical practice, and business acumen and commercial knowledge (CIPD, 2020).[88]

The focus should equally, be on the development of people managers and their learning journeys. Bridging the skills gap at all managerial and non-managerial levels of employees, is paramount. The combined approach of employees, people managers, and learning and development professionals will support the learning, which contributes to the strategic goal achievement in Business 5.0. It requires a collaborative approach to identify Business 5.0 areas for development, resulting in efficacious working, operational success, and strategic alignment. Employee performance enhancement is made possible through new skilling, customising learning events, and facilitating the learning journey of employees. The roles of learning and development professionals and people managers are transforming into that of learning coaches.

> ✓ **Learning journeys, with inbuilt flexibility, customised to suit the learning styles of employees and capturing the latest learning areas and trends, is the combined effort of employees, learning and development professionals, and people managers.**

09 | Talent Management

Strategic alignment, business processes, market segments, and product offerings become the key elements in determining the talent required for success in Business 5.0. The talent areas that need to be acquired will define the type of employees who have the talent mix and those employees who can be developed within a short duration of time or need to be externally sourced. The demographics, psychographics, and talent profile availability that Business 5.0 requires, emanate from Business 5.0 visionaries and their talent assessment.

⇒ **Talent assessment**

Organisations need to determine the current talent pools and the future talent reservoirs they need. They need to acquire the right talented employees and ensure that these employees are ready to perform immediately or within a short time span. Having the business insight, tapping on the experiences of current generations, and capitalising on their technological acumen, customer patterns/demands, and employment expectations, are required in Business 5.0. Assessing the talent mix of the current employees is the first step towards talent management. Talent assessment in terms of:

- Identification of talent gaps and determining areas for development.

- Employees' willingness to develop and acquire Business 5.0 knowledge bases and skill sets.
- Employees' readiness for a mindset change.

This assessment will give a good overview of employees who need and can be developed in their current role or for a new role. The assessment extends to the business functions/projects which they are currently working on, or a new function/project that they need to work on. This necessitates taking into cognisance, the multigenerational talent base and talent mix and prioritising their needs to match them with the organisational requirements. An assessment of current employees' mindset and skill sets constitutes identifying the 'success contributing' dimensions like digital skill sets, Business 5.0 mindset, lifelong learning, mental agility, resilience, forward-thinking, inclusivity, design thinking, intrapreneurial ability, and business acumen.

⇒ **Talent categorisation**

A basic categorisation based on the time, effort, and money to be invested in new skilling employees is useful. Employees who can be new skilled within six months and with minimal managerial effort and financial investment in their development, are high potential employees. These employees contribute towards the success of the organisation with immediate effect and should be right skilled on a priority basis to assume the projected roles and fill in the planned jobs.

Employees who can be new skilled within a year's time, with moderate managerial effort and financial investment in their development, should be prioritised. These employees have the potential to learn, grow, and contribute to the success of the organisation within a short duration. Organisations must plan for their immediate right skilling, for taking up the projected roles, and for filling in the planned jobs.

Employees who can be new skilled between one and two years, with major managerial effort and financial investment in their development, need to be focused on. These employees may be considered as not contributing to the success of the organisation, as in the current digitally disruptive age, one to two years of development implies lagging at a pace that is not in favour of the organisation. By the time these employees become skilled and effective, they may have to renew their skills, as their skill sets would have become obsolete. Organisations would consider them for right skilling, solely based on the individual role and the business need. The categorisation of employees for new skilling is given in Figure 17.

Figure 17: Employee categorisation

Organisations are actively participating in local, regional, and global studies on the skills gap, which may adversely impact business operations and their standing in the market. The industry-education/training convergence is happening on a large-scale basis, and governments are taking an interest in and funding these studies. On the educational front, authorities are validating qualifications and authenticating training programmes based on the skill gaps, business needs, and demand analysis.

Identifying future skills and partnering with education/training providers will keep the external talent pools active, current, and relevant. Business 5.0 leaders need the vision to reimagine business scenarios and talent mix requirements. This vision must be translated into educational qualifications/training provision, as the output (graduates) of these systems will be the input (employees) for Business 5.0. Apprenticeships, internships, on-the-job training, work-based learning, career counselling, and sponsorship programmes would continue to be the steps in this direction.

⇒ Talent portfolios/Multi-specialism

Talent mix and talent portfolios have a shorter life cycle in Business 5.0. Employers and employees need to understand that it is not the loss of jobs that is the concern, but the loss of competencies. The main issue is that competencies are becoming quickly redundant. Employers need to bridge the talent gap by being proactive in new skilling employees.

Recognising the need to move towards multi-specialism will propel organisations in the right direction in the Business 5.0 environment. The younger generation of employees have inbuilt agility and resilience not just in their personalities but also in their mindset and skill sets, in addition to having multiple interests. For employees to be future-ready, they need to acquire a talent portfolio of varied specialisms rather than one specialism. A broader spectrum of talent areas resulting in talent portfolios, will give employees the scope for sustainable employment and employability.

Generalist roles are replacing specialist roles in Business 5.0. One to two decades ago, it was challenging for generalists to find the right jobs quickly. Currently, and in the near future, it is generalists with multi-specialism, who would find the right jobs quickly, as their multi-specialist/talent mix makes them more suitable for talent portfolio/multi-disciplinary, multi-skilled assignments and projects. Single specialism career pathways would still be laid, based on the type of industry, nature of work, customer experiences, market trends, and digital disruptions. As inter-industry and intra-industry collaborations are increasing, organisations are becoming seamless corporate structures, in which having a multi-specialism/talent mix would help employees climb the talent pathways more effectively.

⇒ **Talent ascension**

The shifting trend is in employee career growth and career development aspirations, more so with the younger generations, who may not actually be enamoured by a promotion or title, but with broad-based career development, enhanced professional growth, challenging and interesting projects, and increased recognition. It is not a job per se in the future; it is a portfolio of tasks, similar or dissimilar in nature, which may interest the younger generations. Earlier, it was being a specialist as opposed to a generalist, now it is being a generalist with multi-specialism. Multi-disciplinary choices for job portfolios lead to career growth in different pathways.

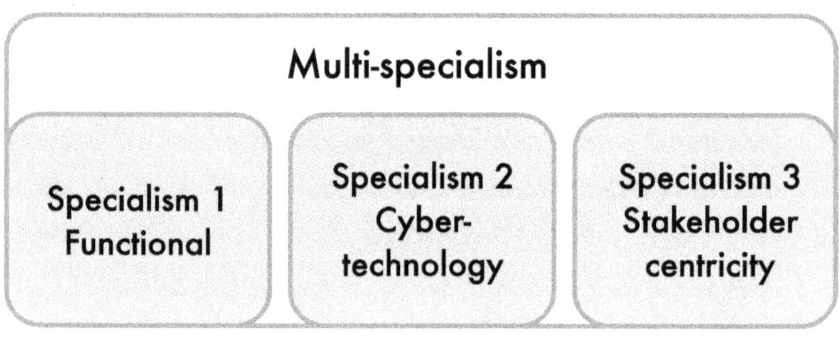

Figure 18: Multi-specialism

On a broad level, the talent search and sourcing are for functional specialism, with a focus on stakeholder centricity combined with cyber-technology skills. Functional specialism relates to marketing, finance, operations, people management, or technology. Cyber-technology skills could be in the form of creating virtual experiences, accessing, and using data for analysis, and operating through online platforms. Stakeholder-centric skills are reflected in creating customer experiences, employee journeys, stakeholder offerings, mapping, and meeting the needs of one or more stakeholder categories. The talent search could be for a combination of these specialisms.

⇒ Talent pipelines and pathways

Forecasting talent for the near future implies that talent pipelines need to be current, and relevant, always. There should not be a shortfall or surplus, the onus of which lies on both managers and non-managers alike, to ensure the **consistency** and **currency** of talent pipelines. People managers need to keep investing in the new skilling of employees to safeguard the talent pipelines from draining out. Capacity filled talent pipelines become a reality with continuous monitoring of market trends, technological disruptions, business advancements, collaborative approaches, and customer integrative solutions in Business 5.0. These key components need to be taken into consideration for employers to support their employees in keeping abreast of the changes in their talent journeys, and for providing trending customer experiences.

Generating revenue, achieving targets, meeting deadlines, and having output, both in quantity and quality of work, are performance expectations that will not change, as this is the foundation that gives organisations a competitive edge. The misalignment in performance levels may be attributed to the fact that the talent profiling/mix of employees is obsolete and the inability or the slow pace with which the management is responding to external changes and factors that are influencing customer experiences and employee journeys.

> ✓ **Talent pipelines have taken on a new meaning in the present era. They are broader in nature to accommodate multi-specialism, and with the flexibility to mix and match talent for a better ascent of employees on talent pathways.**

10 | Business 5.0 Competency Framework

The criticality of the role of people management professionals cannot be more emphasised in Business 5.0. Their focus is on restructuring and redesigning people management systems/processes and facilitating new skilling of employees, so they have the capacity to access technologies and deliver the trending customer experiences. The competency framework aligned to Business 5.0 strategy is a crucial area to be focused on by organisations.

A comprehensive Business 5.0 competency framework outlining key domains that capture Business 5.0 trends, work patterns, systems, practices, skill sets, and mindsets of the C-suite/senior-level managers, middle-level managers, junior-level managers, and non-managers, is required. Competency frameworks need to be designed and redesigned as they are 'work in progress,' at any given point in time. An indicative Business 5.0 competency framework, comprising major competency domains and performance standards, are detailed for C-suite/senior-level managers, Middle-level managers, Junior-level managers, and Non-managerial level.

⇒ C-suite/senior-level managers

1. Business 5.0 strategy domain	
Business 5.0 vision	Visualise Business 5.0 landscape and forecast digital and market disruptions.
Business 5.0 strategy	Formulate strategy incorporating digital transformation by taking into cognisance the Business 5.0 landscape and market trends.
Ecosystem leverage	Leverage the ecosystem for sustainable development in Business 5.0.
Business models	Finalise business models aimed at gaining a competitive edge in the Business 5.0 environment.
Business continuity	Strategise business continuity through risk assessment, contingency planning, and risk mitigation.

2. Business 5.0 leadership domain	
Authentic leadership	Promote value-based, mindful leadership authenticated through people orientation and the inspiration required for Business 5.0 transformation.
DEIB	Incorporate DEIB as part of the Business 5.0 strategy.
ESG	Mandate ESG initiatives to support the achievement of sustainable development goals.
Change management	Lead change through mental agility and resilience for better adaptability to the Business 5.0 environment.
Culture creation	Champion a positive, progressive, and healthy organisational culture.
Organisation design	Decide on operating models and structural frameworks for organisational performance and effectiveness in Business 5.0.

3. Stakeholder value creation domain	
Customer centricity	Strategise for a competitive customer value proposition.
Employee centricity	Build the employer brand to be an employer of choice in the Business 5.0 competitive environment.
Extended stakeholder centricity	Decide on a new value network expected by extended stakeholders that results in mutually beneficial outputs.

4. Talent management domain	
Total rewards	Finalise global benchmarked total rewards that contribute to the IEVP.
Performance management	Promote a high-performance work culture for sustainable development in Business 5.0.
Talent development	Advocate a talent culture by planning employee career development for enhanced performance and employee retention.

5. Learning domain	
New skilling	Incorporate new skilling as part of the corporate strategy for employees' work efficacy.
Synergy creation	Advocate inclusive collaboration to reap the benefits of diversity.
Collective intelligence	Activate knowledge management systems, processes, and methods to tap collective intelligence.

⇒ **Middle-level managers**

1. Business 5.0 strategy domain	
Business 5.0 vision	Visualise Business 5.0 landscape and forecast digital and market disruptions.
Business 5.0 strategy	Lead strategy incorporating digital transformation by taking into cognisance Business 5.0 landscape and market trends.
Ecosystem leverage	Leverage the ecosystem for sustainable development in Business 5.0.
Business models	Construct business models aimed at gaining a competitive edge in the Business 5.0 environment.
Business continuity	Strategise business continuity through risk assessment, contingency planning, and risk mitigation.

2. Business 5.0 leadership domain	
Authentic leadership	Practice value-based, mindful leadership authenticated through people orientation and the inspiration needed for Business 5.0 transformation.
DEIB	Lead DEIB initiatives as part of the Business 5.0 strategy.
ESG	Lead ESG initiatives to support the achievement of sustainable development goals.
Change management	Lead change through mental agility and resilience for better adaptability to the Business 5.0 environment.
Culture creation	Champion a positive, progressive, and healthy organisational culture.
Organisation design	Determine operating models and structural frameworks for organisational performance and effectiveness in Business 5.0.

3. Stakeholder value creation domain	
Customer centricity	Strategise for a competitive customer value proposition.
Employee centricity	Build the organisational brand to be an employer of choice in the Business 5.0 competitive environment.
Extended stakeholder centricity	Create a new value network for extended stakeholders that results in mutually beneficial outputs.

4. Talent management domain	
Total rewards	Finalise global benchmarked total rewards that contribute to the IEVP.
Performance management	Facilitate a high-performance work culture for sustainable development in Business 5.0.
Talent development	Advocate a talent culture by planning employee career development for enhanced performance and employee retention.

5. Learning domain	
New skilling	Formulate new skilling as part of the corporate strategy for employees' work efficacy.
Synergy creation	Advocate inclusive collaboration to reap the benefits of diversity.
Collective intelligence	Create knowledge management systems, processes, and methods to tap collective intelligence.

⇨ **Junior-level managers**

1. Business 5.0 strategy domain	
Business 5.0 vision	Visualise Business 5.0 landscape and forecast digital and market disruptions.
Business 5.0 strategy	Contribute to the achievement of corporate strategy by taking into cognisance the Business 5.0 landscape, digital transformation, and market trends.
Ecosystem leverage	Leverage the ecosystem for sustainable development in Business 5.0.
Business models	Contribute to business remodelling aimed at gaining a competitive edge in the Business 5.0 environment.
Business continuity	Conduct risk assessment, risk mitigation, and plan for contingencies as part of the business continuity management.

2. Business 5.0 leadership domain	
Authentic leadership	Exhibit value-based, mindful leadership authenticated through people orientation and the inspiration required for Business 5.0 transformation.
DEIB	Contribute to DEIB as part of the Business 5.0 strategy.
ESG	Implement ESG initiatives to support sustainable development goals' achievement.
Change management	Lead change through mental agility and resilience for better adaptability to the Business 5.0 environment.
Culture creation	Champion a positive, progressive, and healthy organisational culture.
Organisation design	Construct operating models and structural frameworks for organisational performance and effectiveness in Business 5.0.

3. Stakeholder value creation domain	
Customer centricity	Lead initiatives for a competitive customer value proposition.
Employee centricity	Build the organisational brand to be an employer of choice in the Business 5.0 competitive environment.
Extended stakeholder centricity	Boost a new value network for extended stakeholders that results in mutually beneficial outputs.

4. Talent management domain	
Total rewards	Contribute to global benchmarked total rewards for strengthening the IEVP.
Performance management	Facilitate a high-performance work culture for sustainable development in Business 5.0.
Talent development	Contribute to a talent culture by planning employee career development for employee retention and enhanced performance.

5. Learning domain	
New skilling	Contribute to new skilling as part of the corporate strategy for employees' work efficacy.
Synergy creation	Promote inclusive collaboration to reap the benefits of diversity.
Collective intelligence	Create knowledge management systems, processes, and methods to tap collective intelligence.

⇒ **Non-managerial level**

1. Business 5.0 strategy domain	
Business 5.0 vision	Visualise Business 5.0 landscape and forecast digital and market disruptions.
Business 5.0 strategy	Contribute to the strategy by taking into cognisance the Business 5.0 landscape, digital transformation, and market trends.
Ecosystem leverage	Leverage the ecosystem for sustainable development in Business 5.0.
Business models	Align to business models aimed at gaining a competitive edge in the Business 5.0 environment.
Business continuity	Focus on risk assessment and risk mitigation through business continuity management and contingency plans.

2. Business 5.0 leadership domain	
Self-management	Contribute to value-based, mindful leadership authenticated through people orientation and the inspiration required for business transformation.
DEIB	Focus on DEIB as part of the Business 5.0 strategy.
ESG	Contribute to ESG initiatives to support the achievement of sustainable development goals.
Change management	Adapt to change through mental agility and resilience for sustainability in the Business 5.0 environment.
Culture creation	Contribute to a positive, progressive, and healthy organisational culture.
Organisation design	Participate in modifying operating models and structural frameworks for organisational performance and effectiveness in Business 5.0.

3. Stakeholder value creation domain	
Customer centricity	Provide trending customer experiences as per the customer value proposition.
Team centricity	Work effectively as a team member for achievement of Business 5.0 goals.
Extended stakeholder centricity	Contribute to a new value network for extended stakeholders that results in mutually beneficial outputs.

4. Performance management domain	
Functional/ Multi-specialism development	Develop expertise in one or more functional areas of business, aiming for multi-specialism.
Performance enhancement	Plan for career growth that contributes to team goal achievement and the Business 5.0 strategy.
Performance output	Aim for optimal productivity and work output.

5. Learning domain	
New skilling	Undertake new skilling to be effective in Business 5.0.
Synergy creation	Collaborate and work inclusively to reap the benefits of diversity.
Collective intelligence	Create and use knowledge management systems, processes, and methods to tap collective intelligence.

References

1   Kraaijenbrink, J. (2022). *What Is Industry 5.0 And How It Will Radically Change Your Business Strategy?* [online] Forbes. Available at: https://www.forbes.com/sites/jeroenkraaijenbrink/2022/05/24/what-is-industry-50-and-how-it-will-radically-change-your-business-strategy/?sh=32650ce320bd [Accessed 10 Jun. 2023].

2   Berg, C. (2022). *Industry 5.0: Industrial Revolution With a Soul.* [online] www.clarify.io. Available at: https://www.clarify.io/learn/industry-5-0 [Accessed 10 Jun. 2023].

3   Groschupf, S. (2019). *Business 5.0: Gateway to the Autonomous Business | Automation Hero.* [online] Automation Hero. Available at: https://automationhero.ai/blog/business-5-0-gateway-to-autonomous-business-processes/ [Accessed 12 Oct. 2023].

4   Stern, A. (2021a). *How—and Why—Industry Convergence Is Powering Innovation.* [online] Autodesk.com. Available at: https://www.autodesk.com/design-make/articles/industry-convergence [Accessed 18 May 2023].

5   MIT News | Massachusetts Institute of Technology. (2021). *Advancing industry convergence through technology and innovation.* [online] Available at: https://news.mit.edu/2021/advancing-industry-convergence-through-technology-innovation-0730 [Accessed 22 Oct. 2023].

6   Stern, A. (2021b). *How—and Why—Industry Convergence Is Powering Innovation.* [online] redshift.autodesk.com. Available at: https://redshift.autodesk.com/articles/industry-convergence [Accessed 10 Jun. 2023].

7   How—and Why—Industry Convergence Is Powering Innovation (2021). *How—and Why—Industry Convergence Is Powering Innovation.* [online] Autodesk.com. Available at: https://www.autodesk.com/design-make/articles/industry-convergence [Accessed 22 Oct. 2023].

8   Dixit, R. (2023). *HR Trends for 2023: Future of Human Resource Management.* [online] Available at: https://www.selecthub.com/hris/hr-trends/ [Accessed 7 Sep. 2023].

9   Conmy, S. (n.d.). *What is ESG, and why is it important?* [online] The Corporate Governance Institute. Available at: https://www.thecorporategovernanceinstitute.com/insights/news-analysis/what-is-esg-and-why-is-it-important/ [Accessed 12 Aug. 2023].

10   Thygesen, T. (2019). *Everyone Is Talking About ESG:What Is It And Why Should It Matter To You?* [online] Forbes. Available at: https://www.forbes.com/sites/tinethygesen/2019/11/08/everyone-is-talking-about-esgwhat-is-it-and-why-should-it-matter-to-you/?sh=54f1087132e9 [Accessed 10 Sep. 2023].

11   Andrews, A. (2023). *Council Post: 4 Critical DEI Trends To Watch In 2023.* [online] Forbes. Available at: https://www.forbes.com/sites/forbeshumanresourcescouncil/2023/03/07/4-critical-dei-trends-to-watch-in-2023/?sh=565d287a2f06 [Accessed 12 Oct. 2023].

12   Cornerstone ed., (n.d.). Understanding the difference between reskilling, upskilling, and new skilling. *cornerstone.* Available at: https://www.cornerstoneondemand.com/resources/article/difference-between-reskilling-upskilling-new-skilling/ [Accessed 13 Oct. 2023].

13   TalentGuard. (2019). *Reskilling and Upskilling: A Strategic Response to Changing Skill Demands.* [online] Available at: https://www.talentguard.com/blog/reskilling-upskilling-strategic-response-changing-skill-demands [Accessed 29 Sep. 2023].

14   www.revolutionlearning.co.uk. (n.d.). *The Conscious Competence Learning Model - Revolution Learning and Development Ltd.* [online] Available at: https://www.revolutionlearning.co.uk/article/conscious-competence-learning-model/ [Accessed 9 Oct. 2023].

15   Carucci, R. and Shappell, J. (2022). *Design Your Organization to Match Your Strategy.* [online] Harvard Business Review. Available at: https://hbr.org/2022/06/design-your-organization-to-match-your-strategy [Accessed 12 Sep. 2023].

16 Hecht, E. (2022). *What years are Gen X? What about baby boomers? When each generation was born.* [online] USA TODAY. Available at: https://www.usatoday.com/story/news/2022/09/02/what-years-gen-x-millennials-baby-boomers-gen-z/10303085002/ [Accessed 11 Sep. 2023].

17 Hasa (2022). *What is the Difference Between Digital Natives and Digital Immigrants.* [online] Pediaa.com. Available at: https://pediaa.com/what-is-the-difference-between-digital-natives-and-digital-immigrants/ [Accessed 15 Aug. 2023].

18 Amuno, A. (2018). *Generation Years Chart: 19th to 21st Century Generations.* [online] Parenting Alpha. Available at: https://parentingalpha.com/generation-years-chart-20th-to-21st-century-generations/#:~:text=The%20generation%20years [Accessed 15 Sep. 2023].

19 McKinsey (2023). *What is Gen Z?* [online] www.mckinsey.com. Available at: https://www.mckinsey.com/featured-insights/mckinsey-explainers/what-is-gen-z [Accessed 16 Sep. 2023].

20 Verlinden, N. (n.d.). *Employee Value Proposition: All You Need to Know.* [online] AIHR. Available at: https://www.aihr.com/blog/employee-value-proposition-evp/ [Accessed 16 Sep. 2023].

21 Govindaraju, M. (2021). *Council Post: Rewiring The Workplace Mindset Of Diversity, Equity, Inclusion And Belonging.* [online] Forbes. Available at: https://www.forbes.com/sites/forbeshumanresourcescouncil/2021/06/01/rewiring-the-workplace-mindset-of-diversity-equity-inclusion-and-belonging/?sh=5dc875f821b3 [Accessed 25 Sep. 2023].

22 McKinsey & Company (2022). *What Is diversity, equity, and Inclusion (DE&I)? | McKinsey.* [online] www.mckinsey.com. Available at: https://www.mckinsey.com/featured-insights/mckinsey-explainers/what-is-diversity-equity-and-inclusion [Accessed 15 Sep. 2023].

23 CIPD (2018a). *CIPD | Neurodiversity at work.* [online] CIPD. Available at: https://www.cipd.org/uk/knowledge/guides/neurodiversity-work/ [Accessed 12 Oct. 2023].

24 Kennedy, C. (2023). *Sensory Processing in the Workplace: Practical Tips for Supporting Neurodiverse Employees*. [online] www.linkedin.com. Available at: https://www.linkedin.com/pulse/sensory-processing-workplace-practical-tips-employees-chezzy-kennedy [Accessed 20 Sep. 2023].

25 Verlinden, N. (2022). *Diversity, Equity, Inclusion and Belonging (DEIB): A 2022 Overview*. [online] AIHR. Available at: https://www.aihr.com/blog/diversity-equity-inclusion-belonging-deib/ [Accessed 12 Sep. 2023].

26 Nikolopoulou, K. (2023). *What Is Unconscious Bias? | Definition & Examples*. [online] Scribbr. Available at: https://www.scribbr.com/research-bias/unconscious-bias/#Unconscious%20vs.%20Explicit%20Bias [Accessed 19 Sep. 2023].

27 Masters, T. (2022). *The Fairness Imperative - ADHD and Justice Sensitivity*. [online] Edge Foundation. Available at: https://edgefoundation.org/the-fairness-imperative-adhd-and-justice-sensitivity/ [Accessed 21 Sep. 2023].

28 Wong, K. (2020). *What Is Employee Voice and Why Is It Important?* [online] Engage Blog. Available at: https://www.achievers.com/blog/what-is-employee-voice-and-why-is-it-important/ [Accessed 21 Sep. 2023].

29 CIPD (2023a). *Wellbeing at Work*. [online] CIPD. Available at: https://www.cipd.org/uk/knowledge/factsheets/well-being-factsheet/ [Accessed 14 Sep. 2023].

30 GoodTherapy.org (2016). *The 8 Dimensions of Wellness: Where Do You Fit In?* [online] GoodTherapy.org Therapy Blog. Available at: https://www.goodtherapy.org/blog/8-dimensions-of-wellness-where-do-you-fit-in-0527164 [Accessed 15 Sep. 2023].

31 CIPD (2023b). *Wellbeing at Work*. [online] CIPD. Available at: https://www.cipd.org/uk/knowledge/factsheets/well-being-factsheet/ [Accessed 14 Sep. 2023].

32 Masterson, V. (2022). *What is quiet quitting?* [online] World Economic Forum. Available at: https://www.weforum.org/agenda/2022/09/tiktok-quiet-quitting-explained/ [Accessed 20 Sep. 2023].

33 World Health Organisation (WHO) (2022). *Mental Health.* [online] World Health Organisation. Available at: https://www.who.int/news-room/fact-sheets/detail/mental-health-strengthening-our-response [Accessed 22 Sep. 2023].

34 www.northwestern.edu. (n.d.). *Physical Wellness: Wellness at Northwestern - Northwestern University.* [online] Available at: https://www.northwestern.edu/wellness/8-dimensions/physical-wellness.html [Accessed 23 Sep. 2023].

35 Resnick, A. (2021). *What Is Emotional Wellness?* [online] Verywell Mind. Available at: https://www.verywellmind.com/emotional-wellness-5206535#toc-benefits-of-strong-emotional-wellness [Accessed 17 Sep. 2023].

36 Illinois State University (2016). *Eight simple steps to increase your intellectual wellness - News - Illinois State.* [online] News - Illinois State. Available at: https://news.illinoisstate.edu/2014/03/seven-simple-steps-increase-intellectual-wellness/ [Accessed 16 Sep. 2023].

37 Stride. (n.d.). *Occupational Wellness | Occupational Health And Wellness | Stride.* [online] Available at: https://stride.com.au/dimensions-of-wellness/occupational-wellness/ [Accessed 16 Sep. 2023].

38 Stride. (n.d.). *Social Wellness | What Is Social Well-being? | Stride.* [online] Available at: https://stride.com.au/dimensions-of-wellness/social-wellness/ [Accessed 16 Sep. 2023].

39 Adams, M. (2023). *What Is Financial Wellness? – Forbes Advisor.* [online] www.forbes.com. Available at: https://www.forbes.com/advisor/investing/financial-wellness/ [Accessed 16 Sep. 2023].

40 Menke, J. (2019). *Eight Dimensions of Wellness.* [online] Student Health and Counseling Services. Available at: https://shcs.ucdavis.edu/health-and-wellness/eight-dimensions-wellness [Accessed 16 Sep. 2023].

41 Brunton, A. (2022). *What is Spiritual Health? : Definition & Examples.* [online] Spiritual Posts. Available at: https://www.spiritualposts.com/spiritual-health/#:~:text=Spiritual%20wellness%20can%20be%20described%20as%20a%20sense [Accessed 16 Sep. 2023].

42   www.linkedin.com. (2022). *What is Professionalism.* [online] Available at: https://www.linkedin.com/pulse/what-professionalism-achievemor-inc [Accessed 1 Oct. 2023].

43   Foster, A. and News.com.au (2022). *The surprising origin of the 'quiet quitting' trend sweeping multiple countries.* [online] New York Post. Available at: https://nypost.com/2022/08/02/the-surprising-origin-of-the-quiet-quitting-trend-sweeping-multiple-countries/ [Accessed 3 Oct. 2023].

44   Jackson, S. (2023). *Nearly 1 in 5 workers are 'loud quitting' their jobs, a new Gallup poll says — and it's way more extreme than 'quiet quitting'.* [online] Business Insider. Available at: https://www.businessinsider.com/what-is-loud-quitting-job-definition-2023-6 [Accessed 6 Oct. 2023].

45   Robinson, A. (2023). *Loud Quitting: What It Is and How to Stop It at Work.* [online] teambuilding.com. Available at: https://teambuilding.com/blog/loud-quitting#:~:text=Loud%20quitting%20is%20a%20workplace%20trend%20that%20involves [Accessed 10 Oct. 2023].

46   McRae, E.R., Aykens, P., Lowmaster, K. and Shepp, J. (2023). *9 Trends That Will Shape Work in 2023 and Beyond.* [online] Harvard Business Review. Available at: https://hbr.org/2023/01/9-trends-that-will-shape-work-in-2023-and-beyond [Accessed 10 Oct. 2023].

47   Oxfam (2021). *What is Global Citizenship?* [online] Oxfam GB. Available at: https://www.oxfam.org.uk/education/who-we-are/what-is-global-citizenship/ [Accessed 12 Oct. 2023].

48   McCarthy, J. (2019). *What Is a Global Citizen?* [online] Global Citizen. Available at: https://www.globalcitizen.org/en/content/what-is-a-global-citizen/ [Accessed 11 Oct. 2023].

49   Rinne, A. (2017). *What is global citizenship?* [online] World Economic Forum. Available at: https://www.weforum.org/agenda/2017/11/what-is-global-citizenship/ [Accessed 10 Oct. 2023].

50   Meta (2023). *What is the Metaverse?* [online] Meta. Available at: https://about.meta.com/what-is-the-metaverse/ [Accessed 9 Oct. 2023].

51 Allen, A. (2022). *Council Post: What Is The Metaverse, And Where Should We Begin?* [online] Forbes. Available at: https://www.forbes.com/sites/forbestechcouncil/2022/05/17/what-is-the-metaverse-and-where-should-we-begin/?sh=3c4a084c3e2f [Accessed 6 Oct. 2023].

52 Vulpen, E. van (2022). *Council Post: Three Ways The Metaverse Could Transform HR.* [online] Forbes. Available at: https://www.forbes.com/sites/forbeshumanresourcescouncil/2022/06/03/three-ways-the-metaverse-could-transform-hr/?sh=748fcec56db4 [Accessed 6 Oct. 2023].

53 CIPD (2022). *CIPD | People Analytics | Factsheets.* [online] CIPD. Available at: https://www.cipd.org/uk/knowledge/factsheets/analytics-factsheet/#one [Accessed 12 Oct. 2023].

54 AIHR. (2021). *What Is People Analytics? An Essential Guide.* [online] Available at: https://www.aihr.com/blog/people-analytics/ [Accessed 11 Oct. 2023].

55 CIPD. (2018). *CIPD | People analytics: driving business performance with people data.* [online] Available at: https://www.cipd.org/uk/knowledge/reports/people-data-driving-performance/ [Accessed 12 Oct. 2023].

56 Dixon, N. (2017). *The Three Eras of Knowledge Management -Summary.* [online] Available at: https://nebula.wsimg.com/91a9aa2fdc0e909dc86d3c9f61026d9d?AccessKey-Id=4635E90351C095E6E00C&disposition=0&alloworigin=1 [Accessed 7 Oct. 2023].

57 Kumar Anne, M. (2021). *Key purposes of L&D functions in Organization (Evolved over the past five years).* [online] www.linkedin.com. Available at: https://www.linkedin.com/pulse/key-purposes-ld-functions-organization-evolved-over-past-anne [Accessed 6 Oct. 2023].

58 World Economic Forum. (2018). *World Economic Forum.* [online] Available at: https://www.weforum.org/whitepapers/eight-futures-of-work-scenarios-and-their-implications [Accessed 6 Oct. 2023].

59   World Economic Forum. (2022). *How the passion economy is shaping the future of work.* [online] Available at: https://www.weforum.org/agenda/2022/02/how-the-passion-economy-is-shaping-the-future-of-work/ [Accessed 6 Sep. 2023].

60   van Vulpen, E. (2020). *Top 10 HR Trends for 2021 and Beyond.* [online] AIHR. Available at: https://www.aihr.com/blog/hr-trends/ [Accessed 11 Sep. 2023].

61   Drake, J. (2020). *Agile in HR - Recruitment.* [online] www.linkedin.com. Available at: https://www.linkedin.com/pulse/agile-hr-recruitment-james-drake [Accessed 14 Aug. 2023].

62   Wiles, J. (2019). *Why You Need A More Agile Recruiting Approach.* [online] Gartner. Available at: https://www.gartner.com/smarterwithgartner/why-you-need-a-more-agile-recruiting-approach [Accessed 14 Aug. 2023].

63   Christian, A. (2023). *Workers are quiet quitting, and only employers can stop it.* [online] www.bbc.com. Available at: https://www.bbc.com/worklife/article/20230828-workers-are-quiet-quitting-and-only-employers-can-stop-it [Accessed 11 Sep. 2023].

64   www.linkedin.com. (2023). *What are the emerging trends and innovations in compensation management that you should be aware of?* [online] Available at: https://www.linkedin.com/advice/0/what-emerging-trends-innovations-compensation-management#:~:text=Another%20trend%20in%20compensation%20management [Accessed 28 Oct. 2023].

65   CIPD. (2023c). *CIPD | Strategic & Total Reward | Factsheets.* [online] Available at: https://www.cipd.org/uk/knowledge/factsheets/strategic-total-factsheet/#what [Accessed 15 Aug. 2023].

66   Gaille, L. (2020). *20 Advantages and Disadvantages of a Cafeteria Plan (Section 125 Plan).* [online] vittana.org. Available at: https://vittana.org/20-advantages-and-disadvantages-of-a-cafeteria-plan-section-125-plan#:~:text=Cafeteria%20plans%2C%20also%20called%20Section%20125%20plans%2C%20are [Accessed 12 Oct. 2023].

67   Jansen, T. (2022). *Council Post: What Will Compensation Look Like In The New World Of Work?* [online] Forbes. Available at: https://www.forbes.com/sites/forbeshumanresourcescouncil/2022/03/14/what-will-compensation-look-like-in-the-new-world-of-work/ [Accessed 15 Sep. 2023].

68   Vulpen, E. van (2018). *How Employee Journey Mapping can Change the Employee Experience.* [online] AIHR. Available at: https://www.aihr.com/blog/employee-journey-mapping/ [Accessed 21 Sep. 2023].

69   Nelson, B. (2022). *The Employee Journey: A Hands-On Guide.* [online] Gallup.com. Available at: https://www.gallup.com/workplace/389408/employee-journey-hands-guide.aspx [Accessed 12 Aug. 2023].

70   Indicative. (n.d.). *What Is A Touchpoint? Data Defined.* [online] Available at: http://www.indicative.com/resource/touchpoint/#:~:-text=A%20touchpoint%20is%20a%20point [Accessed 2 Sep. 2023].

71   Vita, A.D. (2022). *Company-employee touch points: how to stimulate engagement.* [online] Altamira HR Software. Available at: https://www.altamirahrm.com/en/blog/company-employee-touch-points-engagement [Accessed 1 Sep. 2023].

72   Baird, R.S. (2023). *Recruiting vs. Retention: Why a Strong Retention Plan is Crucial for Long-Term Success.* [online] www.linkedin.com. Available at: https://www.linkedin.com/pulse/recruiting-vs-retention-why-strong-plan-crucial-long-term-baird [Accessed 28 Aug. 2023].

73   Patnaik, D. (2022). *Boost Employee Skill development by Upskilling L&D Professionals.* [online] disprz.ai. Available at: https://disprz.ai/blog/l-and-d-professionals-skill-development [Accessed 28 Aug. 2023].

74   Global Cybersecurity Outlook 2023. (2023). Available at: https://www3.weforum.org/docs/WEF_Global_Security_Outlook_Report_2023.pdf [Accessed 10 Aug. 2023].

75   Navarra, K. (2022). *The Real Costs of Recruitment.* [online] SHRM. Available at: https://www.shrm.org/resourcesandtools/hr-topics/talent-acquisition/pages/the-real-costs-of-recruitment.aspx [Accessed 12 Aug. 2023].

76   www.cornerstoneondemand.com. (n.d.). *Difference Between Reskilling, Upskilling & New Skilling*. [online] Available at: https://www.cornerstoneondemand.com/resources/article/difference-between-reskilling-upskilling-new-skilling/ [Accessed 12 Sep. 2023].

77   TalentLMS. (n.d.). *Survey: Gen Z in the Workplace*. [online] Available at: https://www.talentlms.com/research/gen-z-workplace-statistics [Accessed 13 Aug. 2023].

78   www.qaa.ac.uk. (n.d.). *Work-based Learning*. [online] Available at: https://www.qaa.ac.uk/the-quality-code/advice-and-guidance/work-based-learning [Accessed 10 Aug. 2023].

79   Digipro Education Limited. (n.d.). *Designing Learning, Micro-learning & Nano-Learning Instructional Corporate Solutions*. [online] Available at: https://digipro.com.cy/seminars/developing-elearning-and-microlearning-nano-learning-instructional-solutions-2-2022/ [Accessed 12 Aug. 2023].

80   Digipro Education Limited. (n.d.). *Designing Learning, Microlearning & Nano-Learning Instructional Corporate Solutions*. [online] Available at: https://digipro.com.cy/seminars/developing-elearning-and-microlearning-nano-learning-instructional-solutions-2-2022/ [Accessed 12 Aug. 2023].

81   Laverty, R. (2020). *Nanolearning: The Future of Learning*. [online] Training Industry. Available at: https://trainingindustry.com/articles/content-development/nanolearning-the-future-of-learning/ [Accessed 12 Aug. 2023].

82   Perna, M.C. (2021). *Small But Mighty: Why Micro-Credentials Are Huge For The Future Of Work*. [online] Forbes. Available at: https://www.forbes.com/sites/markcperna/2021/10/05/small-but-mighty-why-micro-credentials-are-huge-for-the-future-of-work/?sh=7b191593302b [Accessed 12 Aug. 2023].

83   Karb, B. (2022). *Three reasons to use micro-credentials*. [online] UNLEASH. Available at: https://www.unleash.ai/learning-and-development/three-reasons-to-use-micro-credentials/ [Accessed 12 Aug. 2023].

84 Nobels, P. and Baele, S. (2022b). *The ever-growing importance of L&D in the future of work*. [online] www.ey.com. Available at: https://www.ey.com/en_be/workforce/the-ever-growing-importance-of-l-d-in-the-future-of-work.

85 Hayden, D. (2022). *Coaching and Mentoring*. [online] CIPD. Available at: https://www.cipd.org/uk/knowledge/factsheets/coaching-mentoring-factsheet/ [Accessed 12 Aug. 2023].

86 D'Incerti, G. (2022). *Council Post: The Generational Shift In Workforce Culture*. [online] Forbes. Available at: https://www.forbes.com/sites/forbesbusinesscouncil/2022/12/21/the-generational-shift-in-workforce-culture/?sh=4b8e56d0dff7 [Accessed 17 Sep. 2023].

87 Nobels, P. and Baele, S. (2022). *The ever-growing importance of L&D in the future of work*. [online] www.ey.com. Available at: https://www.ey.com/en_be/workforce/the-ever-growing-importance-of-l-d-in-the-future-of-work [Accessed 12 Aug. 2023].

88 CIPD (2020). *People Profession 2030 a Collective View of Future Trends*. [online] CIPD. Available at: https://www.cipd.co.uk/Images/people-profession-2030-report-compressed_tcm18-86095.pdf [Accessed 12 Aug. 2023].